THE EVOLUTIONIST III

COVER ART
Ernst von Haeckel
1834-1919

Ernst Von Haekel's drawings, circa 1850, exposes the similarity of the hands, front feet, fins and wings of different animals. TOP LEFT TO RIGHT- man, gorilla, orang, MIDDLE LINE - dog, seal, porpoise, BOTTOM LINE - bat, mole, duck bill. It is plain to see the five finger skeletal likeness of these nine animals, and no doubt there are many more besides these nine which could be accepted as a good comparison, Today there are both creationists and scientists who feel that man is still different, and endowed with special features which place them above the rest of creation. All creation have, and still are passing through the stages of improvement, explained as evolution. Some of creation perhaps to have satisfied themselves with their present position in life and remain with the same physical shape, while others continue, slowly on the trail of evolution. As emergencies confront creation most seem to adjust if possible, and overcome the problem. However there are some who fail the test. Yet all continue to scramble in their effort to BE.

THE EVOLUTIONIST III
BILL HUTH

HIGH SIERRA BOOKS   2000 AD
KERNVILLE, CALIFORNIA 93238
GOLD BEACH, OREGON 97444

© 2000 BILL HUTH
All rights reserved

ISBN No. 0-9665379-3-9
Library of Congress Card Number 99-094446

Copies available from:
HIGH SIERRA BOOKS
34010 Ophir Road
Gold Beach
Oregon 97444
fax: 541-247-5375

Produced by

DEDICATION

This work is dedicated to a minute list of those who have spent a lifetime involved with searching out truth, as each feels, concerning the time each of creations life-span has been displayed, and to everything that exists in our past, present, and future. Also to those who at one time or another have taken time to gaze into the universe and wonder, "What's it all about?".

Poets, Philosophers, and Scientists

SOLOMON	10th century B.C.
SOCRATES	470 B.C. to 399 B.C. / 71 years
ARISTOTLE	348 B.C. to 322 B.C. / 62 years
NICOLAUS COPERNICUS	1473-1543 / 70 years
FRANCIS BACON	1561-1626 / 65 years
BLAISE PASCAL	1623-1662 / 39 years
JOHN RAY	1627-1705 / 78 years
FRANCOIS VOLTAIRE	1694-1778 / 64 years
CAROLUS LINNAIUS	1707-1778 / 71 years
GEORGE BUFFON	1707-1788 / 81 years
DAVID HUME	1711-1776 / 65 years
ALFRED RUSSELL WALLACE	1823-1913 / 90 years
ERASMUS DARWIN	1731-1802 / 71 years
MARQUIS de CONDORCET	1743-1794 / 51 years
JEAN LAMARK	1744-1829 / 85 years
PIERRE SIMON deLAPLACE	1749-1827 / 78 years

JOHANN von GOETHE	-	1749-1832 / 83 years
WILHELM von HUMBOLT		1767-1835 / 68 years
GEORGE CUVIER	-	1769-1832 / 63 years
ALEXANDER von HUMBOLT		1769-1859 / 90 years
LORENZ OKEN	-	1779-1851 / 72 years
MARSHALL HALL	-	1794-1883 / 89 years
SIR CHARLES LYLE	-	1797-1875 / 78 years
CHARLES DARWIN	-	1809-1882 / 73 years
HENRY DAVID THOREAU		1817-1862 / 45 years
HERBERT SPENCER	-	1820-1903 / 83 years
JOSEPH le CONTE	-	1823-1901 / 78 years
GEORGE ROMANES	-	published 1888-1902
THOMAS HUXLEY	-	1825-1895 / 70 years
OTHNEIL MARSH	-	1831-1899 / 68 years
AUGUST WEISMANN	-	1834-1914 / 80 years
ERNST von HAECKEL	-	1834-1919 / 85 years
CONSTANCE NADEN	-	1858-1889 / 31 years
EDWARD COPE	-	1840-1897 / 57 years
SIGMUND FREUD	-	1856-1939 / 83 years
ALBERT EINSTEIN	-	1879-1955 / 76 years
PAUL KAMMERER	-	1880-1926 / 46 years
CARL JUNG -	-	1904-1973 / 69 years
ARTHUR KOESTLER	-	1905-

Bill Huth
January 1st, 2000

ACKNOWLEDGMENTS

My sincere thanks to my son, Chris Huth, to my life-long friend, Elda Jamieson, to Bennii Worthington - a lady who has spent a lifetime surrounded by dinosaurs created by her father, E. V. Nelson, on the Gold Coast of Oregon, to Ernst Haeckel for creating the cover art, and to the scientists, biologists, and philosophers whose works in their separate fields of the liberal arts have presented me with what they have felt to be the facts of being.

Bill Huth

FORWARD

It has come to my attention, after spending nearly 76 years of life, on what is known as the planet Earth, that the answer to our Being, and to our past, and future, the answer of life, is not so complicated as has been taught to humankind.

As we pass through this cycle, in which we have existed, while being surrounded by others who live in bliss and have no desire to solve the riddle of existence, we all live with the same results from happiness, sadness, health, and illness, each of our neighbors, or cousins of Being, has been satisfied with what has been presented to them. Also, their satisfaction with existence has, so far as I can see, not been effected with the question of, "What's it all about?"! Life, in the minds of those who are not classified as humankind, in my outlook, seem to only present the experience of living. Yet through the evolution of inheritence of acquired characteristics, they too have evolved

Humankind, or those who are able to question life, seem to be handicapped by what is their greatest asset, speech. And the vocabulary seems to keep enlarging. Yet speech has only been theirs, in comaprison to their physical existence, for a very short time. Many, many millions of years have been spent in the production of the method of speech we now contain as human beings. Although not always in the physical shape in which we now exist, and whatever this shape will be like in the future, I am sure that we were, and are now continuously in an evolutionary process. And those physical bodies which we are surrounded by, both seen and unseen, contain the same intelligence which drives humankind. Both or all concerned supply energy (food) to one another through the existence of each other. Through this method of life, mentality seems to be the only benefactor. Therefore, it is up to each to claim their relationship to this benefactor as a means of Being.

BELIEF

Today I am forced, through my understanding, to expose others to what I have learned through my own Being. I fully understand that we are all attached to one another, and form what we call creation, through what we have been lead to be considered as Materialism. The one brain is concealed in the bodies of all. It is the essence of our Being, which drives us.

By understanding this and believing myself to have continual life through the rest of creation, I must try as best I can to liberate others mentally, so they can understand that they, too, are destined to these same benefits. From the smallest to the largest, all are connected and on the same continuous trail of change.

It is not necessary for any of us to force anything on another by using the strategy of fear. All can dream and live life to their own desire. None will be left behind or sent away. Life digests life in order to exist Itself. Evolution presents many facets through Being. There are many pretenders being led by those who conceal their pretentious feelings.

By spending our time as we do, and feeling truthful to ourselves about it, we are in reality preparing a better future for ourselves.

PREFACE

Prefaces, as most should know, are written or spoken thoughts which hint towards an understanding of the material to be covered in the text of the following pages of a book or the spoken words of the speaker. Although the aphorisms I have written on the following pages cover what seem to be many aspects of life, in reality each is connected to the other in a way which explains my personal feelings of how all matter makes up the meterialistic world in which we exist, and the etheristic laws by which we live. This etheristic Being we form is forced to exist on what It receives, which in truth is most, but probably not all It desires, just as we put up with what we receive, which is not exactly all that we desire. The bottom line being; It must exist on what It receives through all creation, and be satisfied with the actions of that which It has created and must exist through.

Although these words seem to fit the situation of life as a whole, I am sure that if everything did happen just as anything desired it to be, it would be a burden to exist in that matter just as it is when things seem to go right and then wrong.

The best we can hope for is to make the best of all that confronts us and be thankful to get it, just as That who created us does, and be thankful to get it, just as It does.

Eternity has always been the point, place, or description of all religious values. Religion lives in the mind as a word which can be used to connect our physical and spiritual selves to life.

As I have professed before, most of my lifetime time has

been spent in search of an answer to the meaning of my existence. This search for any inclination towards generalization which is possessed by the mind of all creation, is the bed of intelligence. Through inclination, the absolute can be reached. Still, the question many times receives an incorrect answer. Yet to put forth, or preach an idea, presents another facet which can be added to create a solution. Without inclinations and their answers, rational thinking could not be. All creation uses limited experiences to construct a dependable answer, which can always be improved. By waiting for all of these inclinations to accumulate before attempting to form an answer, most probably would result in mass confusion. Take one step at a time.

THE EVOLUTIONIST III

THE EVOLUTIONIST III

    Invention and development seem to go along with evolution and in this paper; desire, perhaps, should be included. Invention, development, and desire seem to all tie together in what the word evolution describes.

    When humankind traveled on all fours, it was not wanting to stand up that brought about our becoming a biped. I feel that the reason we rose to stand was the result of our wanting to free our hands, or front feet, for other purposes. Many other four-legged creatures have, or had no desire to raise and stand, or it looks like they would have done so. Perhaps our main reason for rising was that our hands had partially developed fingers, and we were actually using our hands, much like the other bipeds do when they are walking on four legs. Many quadrupeds use their front feet / hands to eat with.

    There were several other things which had to be adjusted before we could rise though, and perhaps the other brutes, who were on all fours, didn't want to go through the problems, or the process to get it done. Mainly, it was readjusting our head on its pedestal, so that when we stood erect, our face was not looking straight up in the sky. Perhaps the way our hips and pelvis had to be reorganized could have also been the reason.

    Invention, or how to do this, might be how it took place. It was redevelopment of what we already had that would take the time. The bones of our hips, shoulders, neck, and skull would all have to

THE EVOLUTIONIST III

be evolved, if we really wanted to stand. Now comes the rub. Did all mankind get together and decide to do this, or was it just a few? If it was just a few, or say half, where are those who didn't feel like going ahead with the idea? Did it look like too much trouble for what they would get out of it? Did they become extinct just because they didn't want to stand up, or was it some mighty power that just said, "It's time for man to rise off all fours and stand up, like the man that they really are". If things were going all right when we were on all fours, and there were only birds walking on two legs, perhaps we were birds, and we got tired of flying. Our nose sort of looks like a beak, and we seem to like sunflower seeds.

    I could really turn this into a full-fledged subject! I'll wait though. It will take too much time right now to develop the direction of the invention for evolution to follow, and it's really not a necessity at this time.

THE EVOLUTIONIST III

This book, Evolutionist III is designed to influence, not through mysticism, rather teaching through scientific explanation how the past came about and what the future of the universe holds for humankind, and the rest of creation. Evolutionist III, along with the preceding books I and II, are books of knowledge created by humanity and dedicated to the scientific approach of understanding. True opposites come together as evolution unfolds the future of the universe, and humankind. No longer are we dealing with only our mother earth. Universal travel is only a step away. It's not merely a question of god creating a planet for humankind, with the rest of creation as servants and food for this creation. Today we are catching glimpses of facts that show the universe to be far beyond the imagination that humankind now contain. Our future can only be truthful.

THE EVOLUTIONIST III

Psyche seems to explain what medulla furnishes. Psyche means breath, principle of life, mind and soul. All of these are unseen, and yet seem to haunt our Being. Medulla, on the other hand is a word that factually describes an organ which is the founding part of brain. Medulla furnishes us with breath, a circulatory system, and the knowledge of life: the foundation of Being, and we can see it.

THE EVOLUTIONIST III

As chaos convulsed, assimilation digested obliviousness into being. Our universe became. Concerned and yet mesmerized. Confusion, time and size were satisfied through comparison. Creation began its climb to be. We were on our way.

THE EVOLUTIONIST III

𝕀 have the feeling that medulla surrounded itself with brain. Maybe medulla is what God is made of.

If this is true, then perhaps thalamus is the spirit.

THE EVOLUTIONIST III

The Evolutionist III is my attempt to illustrate the ability of creation to live as a unit throughout the universe eternally; and to prove this relationship, or connection of one Being to the others who share this existence. And to prove that one can not exist alone. Also, that energy is created both physically and mentally by digesting that which they receive from another. The energy received from another, either physical or mental, is taken thankfully, and in return displayed as a reward to the Being that presented it.

In ancient history, the devouring of another's heart displayed appreciation of the one who surrendered their life. Life itself is a display of those who have been before.

Life, or living, is produced by an uncontrollable urge to be. This desire is as prominent in a flame, rock, water, tree, or animal as it is in the animal we describe as another part of life, humankind. It is true that humankind exists only as a part of all creation. Immobility is not a true display of Being without life. Life, as it is exhibited, is the result of a beginning that will always be. Fifteen billion years, by our time, should at least change the theory to an hypothesis! Soon the hypothesis will be proven a fact with no connection to mythology: a result of an unknown beginning that will always be.

In nurturing what creation desires to be, a conglomeration of beings desiring to exist in peace, we, all creation, shall be at peace, not only with each other, but also with ourselves. Competition will be proven to be an asset rather than a contest.

Assembled together, in one physical body or a billion organs, Being will be used to further the future and give peace of mind to all, as a concern of all. In total, to ultimately make it possible for all creation to fully comprehend that we, throughout the conceivable and inconceivable universe, are on a journey together, and those who created our past are now, and always will be, a part of our future; our life, as we live it. By living life, we will carry on the ideas of those in our past, who still live in the ideas we express for the future. This same existence of those in our past, who still live in our physical and mental future, will be seen in those who carry our, and their, desires for the future together as a model Heaven in existence.

THE EVOLUTIONIST III

Ray Jackendoff states in Bill Calvin's book, How Brains Think, "Universal grammar, or even something like it, appears to be exclusively human."

Have you ever seen a thousand black birds sitting on a telephone or electric line, side by side for hundreds of feet. Without any sign of warning or better yet no sound at all, suddenly, every bird takes flight. How could the message to fly have traveled from birds at one end of the line to birds at the other end so quickly? All of our so-called wild life friends seem to have this same ability to instantly react as one.

Humankind seem to have to see another run first. If there were a thousand humans lined out and the end one decided to run, no telling how long it would take before the one at the other end saw that it was time to move. Which is the most valuable, sensory perception or language spoken aloud?

THE EVOLUTIONIST III

One day, Isaiah the prophet, who lived about eight hundred years before Jesus, was talking to God. God told Isaiah, "Tell your people to put a spade at the end of their spears." When Isaiah asked the reason, God replied, "So they can dig a small hole in the ground to go to the toilet in. I'm tired of walking in the doodoo when I come to visit, and if I step in it again, I'm not coming back anymore!"

THE EVOLUTIONIST III

The inner nature of God displays itself through many colors and physical shapes, but more so through the morals of all Creation.

THE EVOLUTIONIST III

𝔄tmospheric implants are landing on our planet earth by the zillions every instant. They refer to some of these as Cosmic Rays. Maybe they're truly inter- terrestrials.

THE EVOLUTIONIST III

𝕮ompared to the procedure of evolution, the hands of the conventional clock would be spinning so fast that all you might see would to a puff of smoke, as they seem to disappear. Millions and millions of generations, over a period of many billions of years, have been spent in the formulation of humankind as they stand today. And yet our mental facilities, and physical forms still require tuning for what is ahead. As long as our etheric minds, and biological bodies exist, the endeavor will refuse to end.

Eternity will yawn for deeper roots.

THE EVOLUTIONIST III

When someone looks at a tree, they get the impression that the earth is always there, and that the tree is getting taller and taller as the years pass by. In reality, the tree could not be without the earth and its nutrients. It must be that the earth is alive and growing the tree. Lewis Thomas, in his book, *The Life of a Cell*, says the earth breathes just as a one-celled creature does. The only difference is that one breath of the earth takes several thousand years.

THE EVOLUTIONIST III

What makes a plant open its petals when the sun rises each morning, and twists the stem of the flower as it follows the sun across the sky? Again, at night, it recoils to its original position, awaiting the morning radiation of the sun, only to repeat the same actions of the day before. And in the fall, when the sun sets below the equator, fate strikes. The petals fall and stems become twigs. Only in the spring to repeat this cycle as life.

THE EVOLUTIONIST III

It's a funny thing, I never thought of this before. I don't feel we should require proof that plants have brain, because we have already done this through the connection of medulla and pith. However, I wonder if we could perform an experiment, like they do with a high-pitched screaming noise that breaks a glass. I wonder if the plant would survive high-pitched noises?

THE EVOLUTIONIST III

𝔓ardon me. Are you God? Perhaps, if you're not, you can tell me where I might locate Him. Or is He a She? This is Heaven, isn't it?

THE EVOLUTIONIST III

With regard to the soul organ, brain, we have been able to develop morals.

THE EVOLUTIONIST III

I have been asked many times, and probably more so by brother, Gerry, than anyone, why I pursue my search of the understanding of life so hard. I can only say this. My life seems to have been guided and charmed by some one other than myself. I have lived a life of near total freedom. I have had maybe three or four jobs which at most lasted less than a month. I learned the art of hustling near the age of I'd say six, or seven. By the age of fifteen, in 1938, and towards the end of the 1929 Great Depression, when most folks, much older than me, were making twenty five cents an hour, I was making a couple of hundred dollars a week in the muffler business, which I started in the alley behind my mothers cleaning agency where the three of us lived.

When I was nineteen, and just out of the Air Force, I was running whiskey and making a couple of thousand a week. At this age I bought my first road house, the El Rio Club, in Pocatello, Idaho. I learned the gambling business there. Within two years, I took off my first big score, with a partner who had taught me to deal cards and always win, Smiley Brown. We beat a guy for forty five thousand dollars. Not settling for winning money fast enough I then learned the confidence business. As far as making money this was the greatest. Five thousand a week was pretty easy and when I went to Cuba, during the time of Batista's overthrow of Prio's government our take could, at times, be over one hundred thousand a day. It was big enough that we made the cover of Collier

THE EVOLUTIONIST III

Magazine. Kid Mead, a confidence man and partner of Yellow Kid Weil did better, he made the cover of Life Magazine.

The money wasn't always easy though. It seemed to disappear as fast as I made it. They had a saying then, "chicken one day and feathers the next". I used to reply, and I knew what I was talking about after being raised during the depression, "it's better than feathers all the time".

Throughout this existence I stayed as close to nature as I could. I learned that if I acted on my own in any shady deals, I didn't have to worry about some one else confessing. Most of the time, in fact all of the time, my partners were dogs. Smiley Brown was just as silent as a dog. He wasn't much on con, but he had no equal when it came to cards.

When the turn around came I was in Georgia. My partner then, silver-tongued Ernie Dennison, who was just as good at the con as Smiley was with the cards, taught me things about the nature of people that Jung didn't know. At times, we had three or four count stores (short con games). I had spent my summers in the north west, and my winters in the south east for about eight years. When I learned to keep busy most of the year, I had no more problem with feathers. It was chicken all the time. One day the whole situation changed. It was in 1951. I had been thinking about my life seriously and some how got the feeling that if I was this smart I should be able to help others a lot more than just conning them. I told Ernie I'd see him down the road. I never did though,

THE EVOLUTIONIST III

Ernie passed on a few years later.

During these years I understood what I was doing, getting to know how to do it was my problem. I also learned what the so-called honest folks were doing. It was the same thing I had been doing, just a little sneakier. When television got going and the advertising business was getting bigger, I could see a lot of the confidence business was being used in the advertising business.

Sometimes I feel that I was meant to travel the roads just to get a real look at how life is. I knew hard core killers who went to church faithfully and made their contributions just as others did. Many led perfect family lives, while living on the edge of a criminal life. I also knew many dishonest, "honest people". At any rate by seeing both sides of the so-called fence, I could see through most of the guises or outside appearances which made them seem worse to me than my old, hustling, friends. In con talk, marks: for a clear understanding of this everyone you meet exposes to you, what they want you to see. Seeing what they want to cover up is the secret. By letting someone think you are unaware is the foundation of building up their confidence.

One thing I learned for sure, you can't con an honest person who has no desire for your money. To con some one you must build up the larceny most people have deep down inside of themselves.

THE EVOLUTIONIST III

When the ten-mile meteor crashed into our earth in prehistoric times, did it penetrate the crust? It's much different when something hits the earth from outer space than when a volcano erupts and belches flame, smoke, and molten magma. If something would hit the earth, I believe it would leave an open crater, like those we see on the earth's surface. If it was large enough to penetrate the crust of the earth, I feel that the same things that come out of a volcano, would come out of the hole the object had punched in the earth, and would vanish due to the crater being filled with the same magma that is belched out of the cone of a volcano.

THE EVOLUTIONIST III

By studying the process of evolution you will stretch your mind.

By sitting in a Lazy Boy, and deciding whatever will be will be, your mind will shudder, shrivel, and leave.

THE EVOLUTIONIST III

You and I together may be able to gnaw some smarts into the bones of rationalism, and nationalism.

THE EVOLUTIONIST III

It's a pity that science could not have been in front when religious thought came into existence. I once wrote about our ancient ancestors sitting together and murmuring in an undescribable language to each other. One stood up, took a stick, and drew a line on the sand. All of the others marveled at how he had done this. Another stood, took the stick from the one who had drawn the line, and drew another line across the other line, and right in the middle, making an X. All who watched began jabbering and marveled at this great accomplishment.

Undoubtedly, as time went on, many feats such as this were added to the basic knowledge of the bipeds, who were using these as a foundation for their future intellect.

At the same time, there were those who were performing magic and relaying mysticism. It could have actually been a contest for control of the minds of others. Just as today, however, there are those who control with mysticism, while there are others who try to explain things, and how they became, with a factual base. In other words, became through evolution.

Undoubtedly, one of the greatest attempts to put humankind on the right track was undertaken by a young man, Charles Robert Darwin, who was born in England in 1809. Darwin was destined to the clergy as a young man, and his five-year voyage on the Beagle was to be spent substantiating the facts of the great flood brought about by God, during the time of Noah and his family, in the book

THE EVOLUTIONIST III

of Genesis. As a naturalist, it would be easy for him to find many evidences of the great flood, and the first appearances of all things upon the earth.

Robert Fitzroy, captain of the Beagle, was the son of Lord Charles Fitzroy, and the grandson of the Duke of Grafton, and a nephew of Castlerbaugh. For his efforts and display as a leader, Charles Fitzroy had been appointed command of the Beagle at the age of twenty-three. It was Fitzroy who requested that Darwin should join the ship on the five-year voyage.

On December 27, 1831, the Beagle, departed on its voyage. During these five years of being laid open to the real facts of nature, Darwin's mind was slowly being saturated with the raw facts of nature, and the Creationist version of the book of Genesis was slowly being dissolved in his mind. He discussed his new views with Fitzroy, who was every part a Creationist, and whom Darwin could not convince otherwise. However, Darwin used Fitzroy as his sounding board for the new thoughts that he was being exposed to.

After five years of sailing the seas and marching thousands of miles through the jungles and seeing many different tribes of people in different shapes, and bones bigger than logs, beetles the size of birds, and thousands of plants that no one knew existed, Darwin returned home with Fitzroy aboard the Beagle.

Darwin immediately began filing his specimens, and deciphering his notes. Finally, when he was near the completion of

THE EVOLUTIONIST III

his book, The Origin of Species, he began to worry about how the book, with its evolutionary ideas, would be accepted. It was not until he received a paper from Alfred Russel Wallace, who, like Darwin, was working on a theory of evolution and the origin of species, that his worries began to ebb. It was after conversations with Wallace that Darwin offered to share the discovery, and they became very good friends.

A few years after this, Robert Fitzroy took a pistol and shot himself in the head. Many wondered about what had really been the cause of his taking his own life.

THE EVOLUTIONIST III

Most of my life I have worn leather belts. Most of them were, and are, saddle latigos. In my early twenties I realized that if I laid my belt flat on the table it was no longer straight, like it was when it was new. The leather had a definite sag in the middle, or what you would consider the back part of the belt.

I thought this over for quite a few days, and then I began to feel as if I had gotten into a habit, or a rut. I had become regimented. Instantly, I took the belt off and threaded it through the belt loops on my Levis in the opposite direction. I wore it this way for a while and then laid it out for examination on the table. It was beginning to return to its original shape, straight. Since that time I have continued the practice of reversing the direction of threading my belt. All of my belts are staying straight now. I have escaped the results of being regimented.

Freedom is fashioned in many ways!

THE EVOLUTIONIST III

Induction, digestion, action, sleep, excretion.
Induction, digestion, action, sleep, excretion.
Induction, digestion, action, sleep, excretion.
Induction, digestion, action, sleep, excretion.
This is what is known as regularity; even pleasant regularity!
This is regimentation designed for existence.

THE EVOLUTIONIST III

First we had the bisexual. Now we have male and female. Then we got biped. That gave us man and the rest of creation. I can imagine that "bi-life" will be the answer to our relationship with plants, rocks, planets, etc.

THE EVOLUTIONIST III

Which ever you want to live in, security or poverty, you'll have to adjust your own sights.

THE EVOLUTIONIST III

It's funny what humankind can figure out if allowed enough time. I've spent a lot of my lifetime in the gambling business. In this profession, there are many tricks, to take advantage of opponents, which are performed both physically and mentally. One of the originals was used in the game of poker.

Today, when you buy a deck of higher-priced playing cards, they come out of their box, reading, in suit, ace to king, ace to king, king to ace, king to ace, in the four respective suits, hearts, clubs, diamonds, and spades. When cards were first manufactured, they came out of the box reading, ace to king, ace to king, ace to king, ace to king, with the suits in the same order as today. Seventy years ago, when we used to play slap-jack and casino, the cards came out of the box in the original way.

Everyone, no matter what kind of business they are in, try to take advantage of better ideas. Gambling, or playing cards, is no different. No one really knows who figured out how to use the way the cards came out of the box to an advantage, but someone did! Here's how it worked.

A false shuffle, of which there are many methods, is used first. The cards are shuffled, but not really. Then they are placed in front of the player on the dealers right side, and that player cuts the cards. The dealer then picks up the cards, and proceeds to deal.

The game is Draw Poker. There must be seven players in this game, which is the most allowed, and is a standard number of

THE EVOLUTIONIST III

players in poker games. The dealer begins by dealing to the player on his left. He deals the first card off the top of the deck to his six opponents, and one off the top to himself. Then he deals six cards off the top to the others, and one off the bottom to himself. Bottom dealing is easy, with a little practice. Then six off the top, and one off the top for himself. Then six more off the top to the players, and one off the bottom to himself. Then six more to the players, and one off the top for himself.

When the dealing is over, all players have five cards, and each of the players has a full-house, three of a kind and a pair. Six pat hands. Naturally, everyone wants to get all he can out of the hand, so the betting starts off light.

After the opening and betting, no one draws any cards. The dealer draws four cards off the top, jokingly saying he's got no idea why he's in the game having to draw four cards. After betting and raising, the hands are exposed. The six opposing players each have a full house, but the dealer shows the winning hand, a straight flush.

This is the reason for the modern way of loading the cards at the factory, ace to king, ace to king, king to ace, and king to ace.

Another peculiarity in card games is the game of coon-can. About the only place you ever see it played is in jails. If you ever ask if someone knows how to play coon-can, and they say they do, you can figure they've been in jail. When you play coon-can, all of the cards are dealt off the bottom. The reason for this is, you can't

THE EVOLUTIONIST III

see the top of the bottom card, so if the cards are marked, you can't see the mark. In order to cheat, it is necessary to take the top card, and that's easy to catch a person doing. It seems that thieves are always protecting themselves from being cheated.

THE EVOLUTIONIST III

𝔍 mentioned before about spending an entire lifetime in the wilds and never seeing a mountain lion. A few days after making this statement, while driving over the Lion's Trail, between Lake Isabella and Caliente, California, and during the calving season, I finally saw a mountain lion. It took the combination of a road named Lion's Trail and the time when cows are having calves, before I was lucky enough to see one

However, yesterday, during a ride up the Kern River Canyon Road, just a little before I came to Johnny McNalley's Steak House, I saw something that looked different walking along the side of the road. It was about a quarter-mile ahead of me, and going straight up the road. There was no traffic and I slowed down to follow what I felt sure to be a mountain lion. There's something about the way a cat walks that is really different, especially a cat the size of a mountain lion.

When I first saw the lion, I was about ten miles up the river road from Kernville. There were only McNalley's Steak House and another business, The Road's End, in the area, and with hardly any winter traffic, I can imagine that this lion figured it had the area to itself, until I showed up. I could see it very plainly now. All at once it stopped and turned, standing sideways, looking back at me in the car. Then it gave a giant leap, about five feet in the air. Over the willows and down the bank it ran, jumping across rocks and through the water to the other side of the river, where it felt safer.

THE EVOLUTIONIST III

Once again, it stopped and looked back at me. I had driven almost to where it had jumped off the road.

I guess it was wondering what the heck I was doing up here. There was snow all over up high and, usually, when there's snow the road is closed. Now that he/she was across the river, the lion walked slowly up the hill into the rocks and disappeared.

I guess you've got to have patience to see lions in the wild.

THE EVOLUTIONIST III

Most of my life has been spent living around resorts, and most of these were in the mountains of the western United States. I've always been fascinated by all the wildlife in these different places. One thing that amused me most, was to watch the young animals born that spring, and see them become smarter and smarter about eluding hunters and photographers.

One of the best things to watch were the young deer. When they smelled you, or heard you, or saw you, they would run or sneak off to hide. Many times, they would walk behind a tree. When their head got behind a tree and they could not see you, they thought that it was not possible for you to see them, and yet their entire body was in open eyesight.

I guess the old saying., "Out of sight, out of mind," still works for them, too.

THE EVOLUTIONIST III

Evolutionistic views will produce your connection with eternity, of which you are naturally a part of. Again, I say, all have eternity, through the spirit of Brain. It is only lack of understanding that prevents the association of one to all. Like it or not, we are all an equal part of creation. Your existence has very little to do with your understanding. It's only your lack of understanding that prevents you from being able to relax with this knowledge.

In our ancient history, and even today, there were, and are, those amongst us that have taken advantage of the natural things that were, and are happening, as our earth spins through the universe. The lightning, thunder, earthquakes, volcanic eruptions, or other natural disturbances have all been used to make mankind fear a make-believe god that has never existed. If this god were able to do these things purposely, then why should it waste its time at this. It could simply snap its fingers and everything in total would disappear. These happenings are necessary for the planet earth to be.

Yet there are hucksters who continue to merchandise these gods.

THE EVOLUTIONIST III

When you are on the desert, or in the mountains, and feel that you are alone, it is just as easy to feel that there are others, who are unseen, in the area.

It is also possible to feel, when you are alone, that someone is near, and watching you.

Everything has the same feeling. Some, or perhaps many times, both statements are true.

Isn't sensing miraculous?

THE EVOLUTIONIST III

If there was a "Big Bang", and that was the Great Beginning of Life, where did the "thing" that exploded come from?
I know! God's breath.

THE EVOLUTIONIST III

Through the process of evolution, there will never stop being something better.

THE EVOLUTIONIST III

𝔍or the last four or five days, I have been traveling throughout the dinosaur country of northeastern Montana, western South Dakota, and eastern Wyoming. This is not my first, or last, I hope, visit to this part of the United States. Since the age of twenty, I have traveled the roads of this vast high desert country. My first ride across Wyoming was at the age of eight, in a 1927 Essex automobile, on dirt roads. I was on my way, with my mother and a friend of the family, to Des Moines, Iowa. Today, as we are traveling west through Wyoming, headed for Yellowstone country. I am in an Aerbus motorhome on US 90 freeway, with my daughter, Stephanie, at the wheel with her daughter, Megan, acting as navigator, while I am writing this paper.

For the past three weeks, I have been reading certain parts several times, of J. David Archibald's, Dinosaur Extinction and The End of an Era. Let me say, first, that I am not a believer of some of the other articles published in American Scientist and Scientific American in 1990, and authored by Alvarez and Asaro. For those who are unaware, of which there are more than those who are aware, these articles concern the earth being struck by a large meteor or asteroid, which caused the extinction of the dinosaur species. This great catastrophe was supposed to have happened in the Cretaceous age, about one hundred million years ago. Walter Alveraz describes this happening as, "the planet earth being embodied in a similar state to Dante's Inferno". In other words, in a

THE EVOLUTIONIST III

state of fire, brimstone, and darkness. The darkness being the result of the earth being enshrouded in a cloud of dust which blocked out all sun light. For how long, if it did happen, has not yet been told.

If this did happen, it would mean an extinction to most of the life on our planet at that time. Instant meaning instantaneously at the point of impact, and maybe months or so for those on various parts of the planet. No matter where, or for how long, Alvarez wrote, it was all over for the Dinosaur species.

Now, I am going to try and convince you that this did not take place. Around one hundred million years ago there was an animal, so scientists say, which existed under the name of triceratops. Triceratops were vegetarians, which were very large, four footed, with a single horn on the top forefront of their nose, and another horn over each eye. Now if man could evolve through the body of a fish, don't you think a rhinoceros could evolve through an animal that it so closely resembles? Whales were originally land animals. There are many things today, that I feel are the descendants of the Dinosaurs. True, the planet has had meteors and asteroids hitting it since it conception.

Sea shells weren't the only things that our prehistoric ancestors found on, and in the mountains. They found the fossil bones just as we do today. However, they only presumed these bones to be the result of Noah's great flood, just as we are taught. The rising of the great Rocky Mountains, and the Continental

THE EVOLUTIONIST III

Divide, could have been a worse catastrophe for the Dinosaurs. When this happened, the ocean, which covered our entire mid-continent, was slowly forced to be the Gulf of Mexico. Leaving the lush mid-west to become desert sagebrush.

I just can not bring myself to believe that a meteor caused the extinction of the dinosaurs, but the rest of creation survived. It seems to me the largest and strongest should survive, not the smallest and weakest.

THE EVOLUTIONIST III

I know you. You've got to be the one that has existed in my body with me all of my life. You're the person I took into my confidence, and discussed my personal problems with. You're the one that never let me feel that I knew what I was doing. When you first let me know you were "there", I thought I could trust you. Boy, was that a mistake. In fact, whenever I was talking with someone else, you kept whispering to me to watch out for them.

Now you're standing there, watching me being transformed, while all of the little, bastard cells are fighting over what part of me they're going to have for dinner.

I'll tell you one thing for sure, I learned enough this time. Next time, you're going to be the body, and I don't give a damn who it looks like. And I'll be the Soul.

THE EVOLUTIONIST III

𝔉rench scientist Jean Lamarck, in 1809, expressed a new idea concerning evolution. In his profound work, <u>Philosophic Zoologique</u>, he stated, "While the type is preserved by heredity in the succession of generations, adaption on the other hand effects a constant modification of the species by change of habits and the exercise of the various organs."

For all of the phenomena both in nature and in the mind, Lamarck takes exclusively mechanical, physical, and chemical activities to be true, efficient causes of evolution.

Today, Lamarckianism and Darwinism are in full debate as to who is right. I'll have to vote for Lamarck and the inheritance of acquired characteristics, not Darwin, who teaches chromosomes and evolution by leaps and bounds.

Read <u>The Case of the Mid-Wife Toad</u> by Arthur Koestler.

THE EVOLUTIONIST III

How is it that we refer to ourselves and others as having life cycles? Evolution takes place in these life cycles. Trans-formation, figuration, and existence are just thrown in. What difference does it really make how we act or look, as long as our morals improve?

THE EVOLUTIONIST III

Where we think, or feel, we are today, is far from the future we have in store for ourselves.

THE EVOLUTIONIST III

The tides of flesh, as the tides of the sea, shall steadily wash against the shores of ignorance, and then onto the plains of understanding. This understanding will prove, all existing things, in total, form the word God, which we worship. To surrender oneself to be a part of this creation will award Eternal Life . . . by acting out these righteous deeds, which one completely understands within their inner knowledge of all creation, shall prompt their reaching the crowning Glory of Heaven understood.

From the solar energy and through the bowels of this earth, and then continuing up the tower of desire, Being has molded its shape . . . all not perfection, yet all a rung on the ladder of peace and understanding within Its stirring Soul.

As the strong winds blowing across the seas have sent gigantic waves crashing against one another, so, too, have the storms of knowledge sent the flesh of man en masse against itself. And just as the subsiding storm brings peace to a reformed sea, the storm of knowledge brings peace to the reformed minds of men. And as the final storm shall present a complete and shoreless ocean, the knowledge of man shall encompass all things. It shall be known by men, fully, that as I am, so be the other; my desires are the wishes of all. Together we shall mold one another.

Those who have sent their waves of thought into the atmosphere of intelligence have been many. And as these thoughts have pushed the flesh against the crest of others, who are not in

THE EVOLUTIONIST III

accord, a better understanding shall continue to result. These men, who have sent forth their intelligence, are each a composite of what is offered today as a solution to being. Though seeming to be opposites, their paths lead to the same mansion. To please the ebbing tide of man's desire, sets into motion their plan to solve the riddle and give freely what man wants most, freedom with security.

The persons who formulate these ideas may not be the instigators of their propulsion. This, as in most instances, comes from those who have searched the book of life for a way in which they might personally prove their ability for leadership. And with their understanding, they shall pedestal themselves, and offer the idea to those who will listen to their solution to the problems of Being.

From the embryo and its conception, to the acceptance by the masses, the idea is continually polished. The essence, of course, as all solutions, freedom with security. This idea shall perpetuate itself towards the digesting of another, yet slightly older idea which has lost its polish, yet in essence, has the same spirit. With the rituals and codes of these ideas come the zoning of their areas. These boundaries being the results of separate philosophies with the same rewards. Never, in the history of life, has there continued an idea which was not accepted by the multitudes it encompassed. By vote, or by force of strength, what is not desired by the multitudes shall cease to exist.

Humankind, as they are today and as they shall be in the

future, are the result of physical evolution. The elements which compose their makeup are the elements which compose all things. They have graduated, through their desire to be, which has placed them in the position at which they now stand; not as special beings, but a part of life with a purpose - freedom with security. The freedom they own has made it possible for them to move by automation to any part of the earth they desire; yet through the separate ideas of a proper government, they have placed boundaries which forbid their traveling to certain locals . . . these shall soon be withdrawn. The security, which they also own, shall be theirs through the knowledge of the fact that they are a part of Being Itself, which shall never cease.

The descriptive word "intellect" is contained in all Being. None can be stripped of this sense of life. Man, though feeling to be superior, contains only a certain part of this invaluable sense. As certain parts develop in mankind's physical makeup, other parts of these senses are lost. The higher man's intelligence, the more they feel themselves to be separate creatures from those who surround them. Although losing fear of the elements which they now understand, man has come to fear, even more, a simple word they have conceived to describe what they do not understand, "death". It is through their own intellect that mankind have lost their connection with the nature of Being, however, they are coming to understand.

As mankind egresses from the bowels of this planet earth, many physical shapes and shades of coloring are used to protect and

THE EVOLUTIONIST III

promote his continuance. Man is not a descendant of the monkey; rather, man can liken himself to be a monkey. To picture his likeness, man need only picture several hundred humankind, stripped of clothing and with natural hair and beard growth, and living in their natural habitat. To these, add all energy's creatures, from the mighty shrew through the monkey, the ape, the gorilla, the dwarf men, the giant oddities, and then place a blue-blooded queen and king or two amongst them in natural dress, naked, and then try separating them from the rest of humankind. The impossibility presents itself with the fact that very few have ever seen man as he truly is - a hairy, or sometime hairless, mammal.

As the planet earth revolves on it orbits about the sun, and long before the Life Energy had massed into the elements which are at present represented, dense clouds shaded it from the blazing heat of its positive attractor - the sun. Spinning on the slight offset of twelve degrees, and shaded by the clouds, the earth slowly began to cool. With this cooling process, the change of atomic structure slowly presented new elements. And with further cooling, the dense clouds poured their contents onto the slag-like crust. On contact, the crust reacted with huge explosions which sent the slag spreading, and evaporated the clouds contents to reform in the higher atmosphere above the earth. This process continued, until a slag crust allowed the clouds to rain their contents to cover parts of the sphere.

This energy at work is the same Life Energy which is today

represented by a much more settled earth, and also, that "special" thing called man.

As the elements which formed these clouds were sent into the atmosphere, and then through magnetic forces set up by the spinning sphere, we're attracted once again to its surface, and then large bodies of water were spread over the surface of our planet earth. As the liquid made its way into the many faults, it came into contact with the magma far below the now thicker surface. With this contact, enormous pressures were built up, and finally burst their way through the core surface and into lesser pressure above its surface.   With each of these, the surface presented a new appearance, and relocated the earth's ancient oceans.

Slowly, the clouds above settled and the earth conceded to energy's desires, their result; a newly-formed, solid crust which encompassed and harnessed its nucleus energy. Just as today, unbelievable pressures explode and send vibrating shocks along the faults. Gigantic mountains are raising from the ocean's depths, while others are dropping to obscurity. But, as this takes place, the earth's surface presents a new foundation for energy to create and amass its atoms into a new pattern. A pattern which exists in less chaos, and can relax in the serenity of a new born habitat.

Just as the earth has its attraction for the sun, so, too, the elements of its oceans are drawn toward the fiery energy millions of mile away. And these oceans, being in a liquid state, cause the tides, due to their attraction to the sun, as they try, vainly, to stay in

THE EVOLUTIONIST III

its light-giving energy. Many of the elements in the sea have broken down, and their tiny atoms are drawn from the liquid and returned to the atmosphere above.

Long ago, while this process continued deep in the depths of these oceans, a new concept for Being was slowly growing in place. This, a result of a more complex pattern of atomic structure, began to appear on the surface of the ocean floors. As this new desire evolved, it clung tightly to its food supply within these solids, yet yearned also to stay in the light-giving energy which penetrated the ocean's depths, and enabled it to feel there were greater things to be desired, beyond. Slowly, and with these continual desires for light, it tore itself free to stay longer in the Light of Life, and drift with the ocean's currents.

Through this drifting process, it came in contact with other elements, which it digested as it grew into a larger mass Being. Complexity digesting complexity, until no longer was it necessary for the one-cell structure to survive in solitude. A new pattern of life presented itself. A new Being, composed of several different one-celled Beings, presented itself to display a more appreciable way for Life Energy to exist: each profited by the other, who were still performing the one duty for which each was created. As this, and each contributing to the other, the new Being was evolved into a comparison of a small village. Each inhabitant working at his particular trade while the others benefited by his labor, and yet that one-celled Being still exists as the foundation of it all.

THE EVOLUTIONIST III

With the loss of heat intensity on the earth's watery surface, many of the single elements were now existing in a firmament between the earth and sun. And with the loss of these elements, the ocean's surface had lessened to a degree which made it as large lakes which covered most, but not all, of the spinning globe. And while the ocean itself was far ahead in evolving a more plastic Being, the hard surfaces which exposed themselves to the ocean's boundaries were now busily reproducing a new type Being, as the giant plates crunched and tilted as they rose and sank in the magma they enshrouded. Life was being produced from the energy within the solid rock formations, and fed by the manna from the clouds above, life again had a new type of representative.

And with the continual, yet far less chaotic upheavals of the earth's crust, and as the storms poured from the clouds above, both the Beings from the oceans depths and those from the hard surface were digesting and being digested by one another into new and even more complex forms of Life Energy.

The oceans, due to upheavals, were ever being resettled. The lands from the ocean's depths were raised high into mountainous peaks. With each of these, the Beings, which had been torn from their habitat, fought desperately to alter their digestive supply and to be able to retain their existence. True man did . . . but again, with this existence, their physical appearance was altered by the new environment in which they must exist.

Millions of years of continual change, in both the ocean's

THE EVOLUTIONIST III

locations, and the new surfaces encasing the nucleus of the earth, presented an even greater complexity of Beings. Many had yearned to return to the ocean-life, while still others contained a desire to live on the dry lands. Slowly, and just as the desire to Be had come to pass, these creatures made their returns.

Today there exists thousands of species which are very evident of this great change. Sea going mammals, birds which swim yet refuse to fly, alligators which live on land yet travel best in water. Then, too, the salmon, which after being born high in the mountain streams, follows the stream to the ocean and continues in these currents only to return by working a difficult path upstream and back to its birth place. Here, in turn, it generates Being which will reenact this same play of life. As the earth desires to return to the sun, it must stay its distance to exist, for to return it would be digested into the sun's nucleus.

The place of conception and early growth carries a permanent place in the hearts of all Life Energy. The desire to leave is ever haunted by the loss of security. With this desire, a base of directional understanding makes the return journey a complex, yet not hopeless, act.

Dogs have been known to travel thousands of miles to make their return home. The migratory birds annually follow the same meridian lines on their south-to-north journey. The horse and other farm stock can travel directly to their barns after being taken by trailer many miles away. Hundreds of species of birds return yearly

THE EVOLUTIONIST III

to their summer residence and place of birth; the swallows of Capistrano, a shining example. Homing pigeons are carried thousands of miles, and then made free to race to their place of birth and security. Hundreds of species of fish make the same "life to death" journey as the salmon. Again, there are the migratory fish who continue with the warm currents of the ocean as the earth's axis perpetually rocks its equator north and south in the sun's energy. Also, there are the nearly helpless shrimp. Beings which are hardly capable of survival, yet they travel just as the salmon, thousands of miles drifting along in the strong ocean currents.

Far more powerful than the desire to return to one's place of conception, is the desire to return to the conceiver Itself. Man, from the simpler preceding explanation, is calloused to feel they are not any part of the Life Energy, which all creation carries. Yet even more than the others, man's desire to return to the Conceiver could be considered to be of far greater magnitude. However, just as the planet from which they came, with all others who form Being, man feels that to return shall be their ending. But again, in the most dreadful moment of insecurity, humankind will despair at the Being and snuff their existence in an effort to return to the security Conceiver.

A caged animal, after conception in its natural habitat, and then being trapped, and on delivery of the young, will many times devour or exterminate these, due to the lack of security offered by entrapment. A mother, because of this same feeling of insecurity,

THE EVOLUTIONIST III

be it war, fear, or famine, will destroy her children, due to her desire not to create into such undesirable surroundings. Destiny itself can sometimes be felt to be a tear in Being's eye.

Just as the one-celled Beings joined together to bring about their multi-celled predecessor, the small family has joined with others to form the village. These villages united to be a state which evolves to be a nation. To work together is evident in many species of Life Energy. Most pronounced of these is the human race, however there are many, many others who far outshine the Human Being in all-out cooperation. But for the continual conflict of war, man could retain the title of supreme Being on his mother planet, Earth.

The honey bee could be considered as the most outstanding, due to their lack of internal conflict. The ant, of which there are hundreds of strains, is more closely mirrored to humankind. His egotistic frame of mind puts him on the continual prowl for slave labor. Rodents survive through winter on the food stored by their colony. The wolf has learned to travel in packs, which offer superiority over all domain. The coyote, though not commonly seen in packs, has learned it is much easier to trap the prey by chasing it into range of his waiting comrades.

As a single example of intellect, much on the order of man, is the raven, or his near relatives, the crow. These birds band together in their search for food, and security. They are known to place sentries for protection, and also hold judgment for members of their groups who have broken their common law, just as the vultures do. The defendant, if found guilty, is exiled from the group to wander by itself.

The lower primates are controlled in the same manner. Monkeys, Apes, Gorillas, and their species coldly refuse one of their kindred who has contracted disease. They, as sometimes do their close relative, man, use power and strength in picking leaders. The elder of the tribes are consulted constantly for their wise decisions. But because of intelligence being overcome by greed, these decisions are very often discounted.

Due to physical defect and illness, many colonies will desert their kind. However, there are those, too, who will nurse and protect their afflicted.

Relationship of one species to another is always on the minds of those who search out life's secrets. To relate these many forms can be done best by diagraming their family tree to its roots. However, to show the physical relationship is not all that is necessary.

Just as the teeth of many monkeys of the South American Continent resemble those of the human race, the teeth of the South Asian and African primates resemble those of many canines. There are many thousand of physical resemblances throughout the Kingdom of Being. By accepting these, we shall move on to our real purpose, the mental relationship of all Being and its Incorruptible Law.

THE EVOLUTIONIST III

For comparison of these, I shall take the natural habits of the humankind and connect them with each of its outstanding correspondents. Food could probably be considered most prominent as my first comparison. Many of the human species, in reality, are fully able to refuse to eat the flesh of mammals. While others survive almost entirely on it, but on the contrary could survive on vegetation. This controversy has even entered seriously into the religious dogma of survival.

Motherhood presents itself in a very similar way. There are those of the human race who will die in frantic protection of their young, while again many men and women will desert their young in the fear of "death", and many times for reasons of far less importance. This also holds true with the different species of mammals. Age-old sayings can simplify even more this point: "survival of the fittest", "Cunning as a fox", "the memory of an elephant", "wise as an owl", "eyes like a cat", "slow as a turtle", "chicken", "run like a deer", "nose of a bear", "stubborn as a mule", and hundreds of others. Each of these relates the mental make up of the particular human trait to these senses' outstanding examples. One of my pet comparisons of the human and his uncontrollable urge to steal, is with that of the blue jay, or camp robber. These birds, though having not the slightest use for what they may acquire, hide large collections of trinkets in their never-ceasing urge. This can be closely related to the mental makeup of the wealthy, yet uncontrollable, kleptomaniac. The reasoning is undoubtedly similar:

insecurity can not be blamed, but possibly the relating words, possessive security can.

Conversation is undoubtedly the greatest achievement of humankind. Being has skyrocketed its advancement through the coming of this, the greatest of all achievements, to speak a thought aloud to many, rather than the "Other" within.

However, much to man's disadvantage it now seems, here with this greatest reward, man has removed himself from the basic part of Life's Energy, and endowed themselves as the reason for all creation's coming to Be. This thought, with growing knowledge, will disappear, just as it slowly appeared.

On the contrary to what mankind have been taught - all life has its means of physically setting up vibrations which are broadcast to those who understand. Though each of the species have far fewer signaling sounds, these are sufficient to supply them with a cry of warning, the cry for help, the purr of love, or the moan of illness. The bowels of our language are made up of the things we call vowels today: a satisfying ahhh, a questioning eh, a warning eek, a sickly ooh, and moaning uuu . . . as fact, man, without question, was not regarded with all five of these at one time . . . on the contrary, man, as the parrot, is a mimic.

It was not, in my feelings, the conversation which gave mankind time to learn to speak, but rather the period which followed them from all fours to the bi-ped and freeing their hands to scratch and study their natural surroundings. In this way, they displayed their great intellect at that period by also scratching lines in the dirt. With the lines came utterances of recognition. And through the mimicking of the sounds surrounding them, the human race slowly developed their means of conversation. But again, remember, all Being has its means of conversation, and also, that conversation is not necessary for existence.

Mental telepathy, which until a few years ago had been rebuked just as hypnosis formerly was, displayed itself as man's only means of telepathy. With the coming of a more complex vocabulary, our senses of mental telepathy slowly surrendered to a broader means of communication. However, this mental quality is still existent. In rages of fear or under severe weakness, it proves to be a very direct, yet noisy means of expressions. This type of mental telepathy is still the outstanding means of communication with the other Beings which compose, with man, Life's Energy. This silent telepathy, exhibited with physical expressions of kindness, can entertain existence with all that is desired.

The coming of eye sight, another of the rungs on the ladder which leads to the ultimate Being, can be considered also great in our realization. This, just as all other senses, is far from commanding its full value. In this section, my endeavor is to explain that the eye sight of man today is far from that which it shall evolve to be in the distant future.

To develop a single one of the senses by power of self-hypnosis has presented outstanding results. Just as the physical

THE EVOLUTIONIST III

powers can be developed through regular exercises, so, too, can the power of any of the senses be greatly increased by a relentless power of concentration. As fact, this is how all Life Energy has evolved to the position at which it now stands, and continues its progress towards the ultimate Being. However, our self ego will never let man achieve this status.

The bear, because of his very weak eyesight, has a very extraordinary sense of smell. This is the result of one sense being developed due to the fact the others require far less energy. Hibernation, and the act of forcing their face into awkward places for food, such as beehives, could have held back his eyesight. The crow has an outstanding sense of sight and smell, and yet very little ability to hear. Man, when losing the natural sight of his eyes, develops extra sensory perception, and also adds to the senses which are still intact. And, although being unable to see, sets a mental picture in his mind's frame of the way life's objects are pictured to him.

Sun worship, one of our ancient religions, is still practiced in the lands of the Hindus. Those dedicated to this belief spend their existence in the duty of staring at the sun. After many years, these practitioners become totally blind, except for a short glimpse of their idol in the months of its prime. For this tiny, glowing spark, which is witnessed by their burnt eyes, these men devote their entire lives. By this practice, if adhered to by all Beings, the retarding of sight would place Life Energy in a state of relapse. Due to the common

THE EVOLUTIONIST III

judgement of what is best, and not having the almighty dollar involved, man has resolved the Sun worship to be a farce. And again, at one time, many, many millions of years ago, the first sight, which was undoubtedly very near what the Sun worshipers see, was the greatest conquest of Being's evolution: to be able to distinguish night from day. I am quite sure that our eyes were still encased in a film of flesh when we were able to do this. Not fully developed. Also, I imagine the mole, who at one time had full eyesight, lost it due to living entirely under the ground's surface, with no wish, or need, to see any more.

Illusions in sight are very common. The mirage is probably one of the most pronounced of these. Though unvalued, man has continued to present his case as to their reason. Most of us have witnessed illusions of outstanding quality, and through scientific study and natural observance, it has occurred to the mind of man that illusions become most brilliant while the observer is in a physical state of weakness. The alcoholic, with his pink elephants, could be taken as a brilliant example. Or, for that fact, and quite on the contrary, the fasting man, in quest of spiritual guidance. As a matter of fact, it has been my pleasure to witness both observations. And with their results, I personally can feel the relationship of one in the extreme state of physical weakness, is much closer to his reality of life than one who is in top physical condition.

The hypothesis of atomic structure can stand factually beside the power of an undiscovered amount of sensual power. With the fact that the thicker a window is, the more difficult to see through it, my point can be clarified. A piece of clear glass, one foot thick, is difficult to see through. However, with a bit of concentration, visibility becomes clearer; and with practice, the glass will eventually become more and more clear. A blindfold will lose its effect, just as a man's eyes became accustomed to the darkness of the neighborhood theater. As the proverbs state, "All the darkness which exists can not extinguish the light of a single candle".

Although man has not been able to shut out light, he has accomplished the feat of escaping sound. With ultrasonic speed, he has crashed the sound barrier, and can speed away from the sound which is set up by his craft. However, and which is far more important, inside of the enclosure in which he travels, sound is still his constant companion. If removed from this pressurized cabin, while traveling at full speed, the fleshy occupant would be separated from his calcium frame.

At about 600 feet-per-second, sound, to man, has always been a far less difficult barrier to understand, and fully overcome, than that presented by the 186,000 mile-per-second speed of light: for to overcome this presents the fate of disintegration: the return to cosmic energy. A long-held theory of mine has been that possibly the universe itself is formed from a slag of the cosmic Being.

The human ear has shut out millions of vibrating disturbances, which would constantly annoy the mind of its Being. Shrill vibrations, which are set at a pitch which mankind can not

THE EVOLUTIONIST III

hear, are plainly sensed by many other parts of Being. Man, because of his lack of scientific knowledge concerning these sounds and their abilities, has been shrouded in darkness to their facts. Explosions, which are witnessed at a distance, present first the flash, and then the sound. Explosions were probably the beginning of speed comparison, and the first interest taken in their study.

At present, the pitch of the sound seems to have no effect on its speed. However, its penetrating power differs. A pitch set high above man's recognition can cause the breakdown of mass objects. The opera singers ability to fracture glass is plain fact. Also, the concussion of severe explosions can crumble large buildings. Future study of electronics will enlighten Being to now incomprehensible facts concerning sound waves.

As truth, sound, in order to travel, must have a connecting path. This is understood by the degree of speed in which it travels. The condensed mass presents a far greater base for boosting the speed of vibration than the atmosphere of a vacuum. However, sound will travel much farther in areas with less mass atmosphere. To shut out sound entirely is another of man's incapabilities, for to make such a thing as a complete vacuum is an impossibility.

The fact of smelling is, in actuality, the digesting of smell, or food particles, which are carried aloft by the atmosphere. These particles, though unseen by the eye, if concentrated in mass, would form a solid food. The air, which we feel we are breathing, is, in reality, being digested by our lungs and the chaff is being exhaled.

THE EVOLUTIONIST III

Taken in as a necessity to Be, man exhales a carbon dioxide gas which, in turn, is digested by plants, who in turn breath, through permeation, the carbon dioxide and exhale, by the same method, oxygen. Just as man thrives partially on what he breathes, there are much smaller parts of Life's Energy which exist entirely on the gases which travel through what man can not detect - the atmosphere. There are organisms deep in the oceans which live partially on the sulpher compounds that are being ejected from the ocean's floor.

In all actuality, when persons fast in respect of their religion, they are not in complete accordance with their belief. They are still digesting the unseen food of the atmospheric ocean in which they are existing.

The constant radiation of Life's Energy emits from all Beings. The sun, our principle source, emits this energy with such intensity that if the planet earth were to cease revolving, its exposed side would scorch to bare rock. However, with this revolving, the energy is distributed at intervals which create, rather than destroy . . remember, though, that to destroy only creates another faction.

This continuous heating and cooling, which causes expansion and contraction, is the process which brings about the breaking up of the exposed boulders and smaller rocks, just as freezing and warming will crack the cast iron engine block in your car, if it is not properly supplied with anti-freeze. A single rock, if left in this energy, will eventually break down to the sands of the

THE EVOLUTIONIST III

desert. The sands, which are the result of the complete breakdown of the rocks, are swept unceasingly by the winds, which are also a result of the heating and cooling cycles or process, and this sand, which is blasted against the energy which thrives on the intervals of the sun's energy, is gradually worn away into the atmosphere to free once again the cells of life.

Deposits of radioactive mineral are sparsed throughout the crust of the earth. This crust, which seems to average seventy-five miles in thickness at the present time, is steadily growing thicker and thicker. As the earth's energy is devoured from its nucleus by this crust, it is again digested by the surface energy which sends it on into the atmosphere, where it once again begins the process of massing. This theory could be related to the fact that not a thing exists which is motionless: an arrow, shot straight in the air to land at the point from which it departed, has never ceased to move since leaving the bow, and though traveling in a straight line, it has made a cycle.

Molecules, which are formed by the massing of elements, no matter how many times they are split, will remain the same material. For example, two parts of hydrogen and one part oxygen make one molecule of water. This water, say one drop, no matter how many times it is divided in half, will continue to be water. However, remove any of the three elements, and it will cease to be water.

This is the exact way in which energy itself creates and transforms uranium. This very radioactive element emits particles of its composition until it gradually changes to lead. The transpiring of the period of change is the period of energy. The negative and positive poles of a battery are perfect examples of energy. Either pole, negative or positive, is useless by itself. Neutrality itself turns into energy with the digestion of the positive pole by the negative pole, or viceversa. As fact, nothing can exist with out its opposite.

Generation of species, or prostration, or better yet convulsion, of energy is even more complex, and could be considered as the solution of Being. The result of the contact of the negative and positive poles creates and emits from their touching. The creation, too, of new aspects of thought is the digesting of opposing theories. The earth has the north and south pole which travel in opposite directions. The theory of the cowlick in a man's hair and the fact that it always forces the hair to make a clockwise spiral, has been investigated, and is now found that a person who is born south of the equator, which travels in an opposite direction causes the hair to spiral in a counter-clockwise direction.

Prostration takes place in many millions of ways, and with the evolving of the species, will continue to present new cases. Mankind conceives during the impact of their greatest physical explosion of energy. This same holds true for all energy, and the prostration before conception is just as climatic, and requires relatively the same physical strain for each species of Being, be it physical or mental.

The prostration of Energy, in Its conception, is a continual

THE EVOLUTIONIST III

process. As the earth swings on its axis, the relative exposure to its sun-given energy presents a never-ending stream of birth from their species. Many exist for hundreds of revolutions of the earth, as it orbits around the sun; many more exist for millions of revolutions. Again there are those which exist for a few hours in the afternoon, and, too, there are those Beings which exist only momentarily. The earth, being a product of Energy, has its own span of existence. The force behind Being is to Be Itself: the reason for evolution is to reach the infinite in what to Be.

In an effort to explain certain periods, man has taken the word, generation, as a means of approximating that period of time; or by saying this younger generation is not like our generation. The word, generate, means a continual flow of energy. To liken it to a period of time would, as matter of fact, be to liken it to an instant so small, that a second would be as a year. Generation, when including a period, can only be contemporary. However, generation, when including a mass, can only mean the amount born at that particular instant. Generation of species, as fact, is like the ceaseless change of the oceans floors.

Mankind now stands at the threshold of presenting the answer to many dreams. With the completion of space craft, man will visit other continents in the Universal Sea. Not only have they succeeded in the conquest of knowledge, they are making it possible to carry forward the monument, Man Being, to stride forward from where he now stands, and eliminate evolving, once again from the

THE EVOLUTIONIST III

chaos of conception, to where he now stands.

Just as the bee carries the pollen of the flowers, man shall carry the pollen of earth; not only physical pollen, but mental pollen, for soon we shall know that the thoughts embedded in the minds of our future generation are far more powerful than any conception that physical energy has yet presented.

Philosophy has extended itself into many fields. And, as always, philosophy has attempted to present a pathway to righteousness. Theology, or Godly discourse, seems to be the root of philosophy, and the nucleus of this sort of conversation.

With each philosophy has come a meaning, and another way of unfolding what has always existed, but only lacked explanation. And, too, this explanation only reached a minority, who were capable of explaining the essence of its thought. Many, undoubtedly, who have tried, have only bungled what may have been a valuable explanation as to the question of being. But, because of their concept of the particular philosophy, which they are promoting, it was disregarded and lost before it could bury its roots - or yet, because it could not blossom its pollen: for, in essence, all philosophy is tended by the same Gardner.

A simple, yet very positive, thought is the ancient philosophy of Mazdaism. In respect of this, we have one of the great discoveries of Being. As a shining example, the Mazda electric light bulb. This philosophy is positive and creative, and expresses Itself through all religion; in order to have black, you must have white; in order to have love, you must have dislike; in order to have cold, you must have heat; in reality, in order to know one thing, we must understand the opposite; and in finality, in order to understand what we feel to be right, we must first understand what we feel not to be right. To others, these rights and not rights might be in opposites. This places upon you the problem of decision. You understand, under certain circumstances, what is right to you and what is not. You are, at this time of choosing, the emissary of the highest possible seat which Being affords. In reality, you are acting as what we have no right to be, according to the Old Testament, a Judge. The moral is to judge what you feel, truthfully, is right.

To build a new understanding, one must first falsify the existing thought, which has been taught as fact, and then pronounce what you feel to be right judgments. In the case of the noun (and we must call it that) "death", it has been used to express the change from present to future life. However, it would be more fitting that this word be used for that period of time which lapses in alternating current. "Death" has been the axe of the vicious since creation came to Be. In this I mean, to be used as a means of holding mankind in the clutch of fear and ignorance. Energy continues, life progresses. With full understanding will come Heaven understood.

To explain the word "death', we must do more than read the dictionary. Its meaning best would be to denounce the thought "dead". Dead explains something which is inanimate or motionless.

THE EVOLUTIONIST III

Science will prove nothing is motionless. In order for something to be "dead", it can not be. Here you might say, "John is dead". But the mention of John to yourself, brought John to life in your own mind, or the minds of those who might have been listening. What has been seen, can never be lost.

If an element can expend energy, and slowly be changing into another, could not all of creation proceed in the same direction?

THE EVOLUTIONIST III

Evolution constitutes Christianity, the words of Jesus, and the prophets; in a factual, truthful manner. When one says, "Treat your neighbor as a brother, or yourself", he is rightfully telling you what evolution equals. Evolution is your future and your past: it's God's will.

It is impossible to believe that the bodies of all creation are inferior to humankind. God created them all, and continues to do so. It is only to discover the truth of equality, more so with ourselves than with others. Equality, in reality, presents no problem.

THE EVOLUTIONIST III

If you keep your mouth shut, you can think.
If you can't, then listen.

THE EVOLUTIONIST III

Through the mind, we really become One.

THE EVOLUTIONIST III

𝕲enesis, chapter five. The genealogy of Adam started with Adam, himself. God made Adam out of dust and then removed one of Adam's ribs and created Eve. God, Himself, is the only one who knows what Adam and Eve looked like. I guess that is not right either because the serpent knew both of them and he told Eve it was okay to eat from the tree that let them know right from wrong. Evidently serpents had a language at that time, and Eve knew it.

Anyway Adam and Eve had Cain. And then they had Abel. Cain killed Abel and then the Lord, who I guess is still God, got mad and ran Cain out of town. Cain left Eden and hiked over to Nod, a little east of Eden.

Some how Cain got a wife. It doesn't explain how but they had a kid called Enoch. Then Enoch mated with some unknown woman and she gave birth to Irad. Irad then with some other woman had Mehujael. Mehujael begot Methushael. Now Methusael's wife had Lamech. Lamech took himself two wives.

I really have no idea where all of these wives came from unless God found a bunch of ribs some place and created them. Anyway I guess we'll just have to take Moses' word for all of this, he was the one that wrote the book, with a little help from his brother Aaron. Aaron knew magic too. Maybe that's where all the ribs came from.

Back to the action. Lamech's wives even had names, Adah and Zillah. I'll bet they were killer-dillers. Adah then had Jabal and

THE EVOLUTIONIST III

Jubal. As for Zillah, she also bore Tubal-Cain. And the sister of Tubal-Cain was Naamah.

Adam and Eve then had another son, Seth. He, too, had more sons and daughters. Now we're getting some place. We're getting some daughters for wives. Enos begot Cainan, then Enos had more sons and daughters. Cainan then had Mahalaleel. And then Cainan had sons and daughters. Mahalaleel had Jared, and Mahalaleel had sons and daughters.

This goes on for a few more generations, and then Lamech II had Noah. And this is very interesting; Noah lived five hundred years, and then had Shem, Ham and Japeth.

Now it gets really interesting, when men began to multiply on the face of the earth, and daughters were born to them. Soon, the sons of God (I thought Jesus was the only son of God, oh, that's right, Jesus was begotten) saw the daughters of men. How about that, the daughters were only the daughters of men. What a deal, the sons came from God and the daughters only came from men.

Now God began to see that the men He had created were messing around with the women that the men had, and that even the earth was beginning to become corrupt. (chapter six, verse eleven) So He, God, told Noah to build an Ark.

Then He, God, told Noah (chapter six, verse 19) that all the birds, animals, and every creeping thing, two of every kind, will come to you to keep them alive. Then in chapter seven verse two

THE EVOLUTIONIST III

God changed his mind. He told Noah to take seven of the clean animals and only two of the unclean animals and seven clean birds and only two of the dirty birds. This whole thing is too much! And to top this off, you should see the artist's conception of the Ark. It's pitiful that some folks still believe this, and worse than that, they teach it to their kids as truth.

So God drowned everyone else, and Noah set sail.

THE EVOLUTIONIST III

Long, long ago, when we were only in the form of plants, we were almost immobile. When I say almost immobile, by that I mean our only method of moving was as the Ivy grows. Even though the roots are in one place, the Ivy can grow towards where it wants to be. Not very fast, but at least it gets there. When God saw how determined the Ivy was, God put it through the evolutionary process, and after traveling so far, God made it possible for Ivy to grow another set of roots, and take off for another destination, After so much of this, the Ivy decided to go home. There was no problem of getting lost, it just followed its own stems.

THE EVOLUTIONIST III

My brother, Gerry, in World War II, worked on the Lido Road in China. Burma was the nearest town. If a native got into a truck, who had never been in, or on one before, and the truck was traveling at a high speed, the native would just step out and off the truck. Once they hit the ground, they knew they had made a mistake. It didn't take long for them to learn.

Learning is what it's all about, that's evolution.

THE EVOLUTIONIST III

Our problems are not presented by God. On the contrary, we have generated and raised them ourselves. The longer we leave them lay, the larger they grow. It's much easier to flush them from our system by exposing them to others of our own species, while they're young.

THE EVOLUTIONIST III

What you believe has nothing to do with what happens to you. It's what you desire that makes the difference!

THE EVOLUTIONIST III

Radiata, Mollusca, Articulata, and Vertebrata are the basic names concerning Being which were used by Cuvier. Radiata, a result of friction, Mollusca, a conglomeration of flexible, fleshlike jello, Articulata, a directional being, Vertebrata, the advancement of the three to the limits in all species. Though these four were the representative of basic life, they all contained the same material in their make up. It was a matter of fact that the differences in the elements each contained, and the evolutionary design which followed their creation, God left no vacancies.

In our Earlier attempts to define the makeup of man, we naturally were groping in the dark, and using our past discoveries as a foundation for discovering more information of the beginning of man. One of Matthia Schleiden's (1838) early discoveries was the shape of the cell of the plant world. There was one common element of all the different cell tissues. This common element was and still is contained in both plant and vertebrate. In fact in all life including rock. This cell is contained in both pith of the plant stem, vertebrate, and algae which blossoms from rock. It is basically a part of brain, which is supplied in all creation.

Rock placed in water, or watered every day will transform to algae, life in the minute stage.

After Schleiden's discovery Johannes Muller discovered the same cell tissues to be in the animal world. Schleiden, Schwann, Kolliker, Muller and Virchow all arrived at this same result.

THE EVOLUTIONIST III

Elementary organisms also led to discoveries which were proof that brain, the instrument of consciousness, and all of the higher functions of the mind, by its construction and size present very many variations in detail, but its basic characteristic structure remains always the same. The next time you see a rock be sure to say hello!

THE EVOLUTIONIST III

What is it with cattle? Certain species of cattle, it seems, have no fear of man. There seems to be a question in their mind, but they continue to stand quietly and chew their cud as a person approaches them.

There must have been something sacred about cattle in our prehistoric past. We must have learned to protect them rather than to bring them to extinction. Undoubtedly, they have been around for thousands and thousands of years. Evolution had to be a part of their being, but nothing much seems to be mentioned of their history.

At least, during their beginning, mankind had enough intelligence to protect an easy source of fuel, for their cave man bodies.

THE EVOLUTIONIST III

One day, I was watching a cow lean against a telephone pole, and it commenced rubbing against the pole. I could see the satisfaction in its eyes as it kept scratching its itch on the pole. While I sat there watching, I began to wonder about how all creation seems, at sometime, to have to scratch. I can really feel this when I see a snake that is in the middle of shedding its skin. I'll bet the snake must really be itchy at that time.

You know what I really wonder? I wonder what it is that seems to make us feel that we are different.

THE EVOLUTIONIST III

The cells, organs frame, and flesh of your body, since its conception, have passed through most of the natural steps of evolution, from the cell to the full force Being.

All of this takes only nine months, and sometimes less. It took millions of years to produce this process!

THE EVOLUTIONIST III

There's always a counterbalance, both physical and **mental**.

THE EVOLUTIONIST III

The first stimulus into the human frame arose through illness. Naturally those who were most confronted, in our early stages of existence, were those who had the problem. The answer to the problem of the illness was definitely trial and error. It was sometimes simple to answer the problem of the illness if it concerned something eaten. Sour or bitter objects were the first to go, this automatically avoided many stomach problems. Tooth aches must have been a grin and bare it situation. Broken bones just healed. Setting them undoubtedly came thousands of years later.

In the days when the Jewish religion was first organized, the followers were ordered to bring any livestock to the priests to be slaughtered. During the slaughter the blood was sprinkled about the alter and certain parts were burnt as a sacrifice to their god. After the slaughter was completed, along with the sacrificial rights the priests were given some of the meat and the rest was taken by the owners to their camp. Before leaving the alter, they were ordered to only eat the flesh of the beast for three days. If there was any left after the three days it was to be offered as a burnt offering to their god. The reasoning for this burnt offering was that if they didn't burn it as an offering to God, God would condemn it and it would make those who ate it on the forth day ill. The true reason was understood by the priests, they knew the meat would spoil in three days cooked or not.

For those who had no priests, but were using the method of

THE EVOLUTIONIST III

basic science, the meat was dried, smoked, brined, or salted to overcome the waste of a burnt offering to a non-existent god who would purposely cause illness if he wasn't given the burnt offering in three days.

THE EVOLUTIONIST III

Some say a nightcrawler does not have brain. I fish with nightcrawlers, most of the time. When I'm ready to put the nightcrawler on the book, I take him by the tail and swing it around, and then hit his front part, which I consider to be the head, on my knee. When this happens, the nightcrawler shrinks in length, and swells in diameter, and sort of quivers. This action, to me, would show that the nightcrawler does have brain, or why would this reaction display itself, and then, in a minute or so, go away, and the nightcrawler returns to normal?

The reason for my doing this to the nightcrawler is that it is much easier to place the hook in the nightcrawler when it is stunned, and also being unconscious relieves the pain of the hook entering his body.

How would I be causing this reaction, if the nightcrawler did not have brain? It couldn't be the nervous system. Nerves alone cannot report a problem, they must have brain to report to.

THE EVOLUTIONIST III

The Giant Squid, which lives in the deepest parts of the Pacific Ocean, is an invertebrate animal. This seems, to me, to mean that they are boneless. If my calculations are correct, this would mean that they have no spinal chord, because they have no backbone or rib cage. With neither of these, they are still equipped with brain. Some scientists teach that brain is formed on the tip of the spinal chord. If this is true, then a squid should not be able to have brain, because they have no spinal chord. Yet they do have brain.

THE EVOLUTIONIST III

Confident anticipation. These two words describe what the confidence man wants his mark to visualize in his, the mark's, lust for wealth, or to satisfy his ego.

THE EVOLUTIONIST III

𝕶now yourself to be what you see in others!

THE EVOLUTIONIST III

𝔅rain seems to be much like a container for electricity. We have to recharge it with sleep. This charge only lasts so long and then sleep is the only means by which we can recharge it. Without sleep, brain will soon lose control and explode our bodies into rage. A different sort of reaction takes place when our bodies receive no food to create blood which furnishes, or supplies oxygen to brain. Results from energy not being supplied by food being digested into blood for brain come in the form of hallucinations, or visions, dreams, or milder types of brain activity. If oxygen is not supplied, or the blood stream is cut off brain suffocates.

Through the study of these thoughts we can surmise then that oxygen seems to be the main food for brain, just as it is for the lungs and gills of bodies which are used by all creation. Being seems mainly to be the result of oxygen. If this is true then we might consider the study of how this life giving oxygen might be affecting the soul or spirit.

Another theory, or thought, could be that oxygen and friction (electricity) could be the result of the creation of soul and spirit. Also we might mix in a little magnetism. All three are unseen. Yet we know they exist. Even more so than the soul and the spirit.

Everything seems to require orders to keep on track. Perhaps this is where another, unseen God comes on the scene.

I'll continue reading and digesting. These results also seem to come from nowhere. And just as creation is being constructed to become a physical fact and resolves back into etheric dust, so too the soul and spirit are being constructed and they dissolve or neutralize to nothing, only to be reconstructed or reconstituted. If these things happen to the physical and the unseen it is also possible that we, who live throughout creation in physical bodies, transpire constantly; with slight changes as we return. It's only a matter of comprehension; however, I'm sure we do!

THE EVOLUTIONIST III

𝕴f you are humankind, then you should be able to read the words on this paper, and, possibly, you will understand them. If you feel you would like to understand more of life, look into the eyes of all who surround you. This is only the beginning. Watch the light of day turn to darkness. Why is it that space is light and shade makes a shadow, but darkness has no shadow? Or perhaps let your mind tell you why you have compassion.

All creation asks, Why? Why is it that we have to struggle to exist, when we know that, soon, existence will be automatically taken from us in the physical form we now wear? Why is it that there are ups and downs in our mental senses, and yet we have done nothing to bring these feelings to the surface? Why is it that before we sleep, we are many times in low spirits, and then awake in the morning cheerful?

What takes place in our sleep that is magic enough to change our outlook on life? Is it because sleep causes the callous, which enshrouds our problems? Why is it that sleep does not conceal happiness? Is there a difference?

Tomorrow morning, you will understand the reason. It will not be the same answer for all, due to the fact that each press themself into the position of certain ways of feeling.

THE EVOLUTIONIST III

At the present time I'm reading, <u>At the Water's Edge</u>, by Carl Zimmerman. He states on page 202, "Along with the early Sirenians, these were probably the first mammals to give birth to a breathing baby under water."

If the young don't have brain, how is it that they have the sense, upon birth, to immediately swim to the surface for a breath of air, or climb to the pouch of an opossum or kangaroo for milk?

I really don't understand how a whale, after millions of years of being a mammal on land, and, giving birth to their young on land, can work their way into a life in the water and give birth in the water to an air breathing mammal. There must be some intelligence in babies that makes the impossible, possible.

THE EVOLUTIONIST III

If our fuel for our vehicles ran out, our real reward would be to be able to see and breathe clean air again.

Sometimes I feel that having comforts are worth seeing less, but we can't breathe less.

Everything has its way of living.

THE EVOLUTIONIST III

I've been died on so many times, that I no longer have pets, and I don't like making new acquaintances, only to lose them. I seem to feel better if I never knew them in the first place.

THE EVOLUTIONIST III

We speak of the universe coming into being. Massive tornadoes, a big bang, or a sudden appearance of something coming out of nowhere. I, myself, feel that the creation of our universe is still in the same process or construction, just as all creation is. With no major or minor mentality levels. This process of building this universe with one part being constructed while another part is being eliminated is the same thing that all of creation goes through, with no ending.

These same rules of construction and elimination seem to pertain to the creatures which inhabit the universe as much as the universe itself. Both of these statements might be considered as fact, both concern physical objects which we can focus our eyes on.

Soul and spirit seem to tell us of something that is here, but we are unable to physically see. We can only say it exists. Much like the oxygen we breathe, even more we know that oxygen exists, because we can produce it. We can separate it from the atmosphere, and compress it, by forcing it into tanks under great pressure and use it as we need it. Still, we are unable to see it. Could it be then that which our spirit and soul are made of, and which we cannot see, in some way might be harnessed. Take a "look" at electricity. It is also unseen, except in lightning, and sparks, yet it is here. We construct many canisters which are used to contain it, yet it can only be known by the energy it dissipates which goes back into the atmosphere, or escapes by permeation through anything we construct to contain it.

THE EVOLUTIONIST III

It must be used before a certain time just as the limits of containment, time, is stamped on the batteries we use. Our progress with electricity is improving daily. The charges and containment are lasting longer, and the canisters are becoming smaller.

Perhaps, in the near future, we will be able to compress and contain other sorts of natural energy. Come to think of it, we already do. Here, have a benzedrine tablet.

THE EVOLUTIONIST III

Immaterialism is the doctrine that matter does not exist of itself as a substance or cause, but that all things have been, or are seen to have existence through the ideas or perceptions of a mind. Again we must take into consideration the words of George Berkeley, "The Immaterialists of modern times (1822-29) freely admit that the mind has no place of existence. Friction and magnetism seem to possess equal claims with thought to the unmeaning distinction of immateriality."

The words of Robert Louis Stevenson, spoken through the mouth of Doctor Jekyll, properly described the truth of Immaterialism, "The trembling immateriality, in which the mist-like transience of this seemingly so solid body in which we walk attired."

THE EVOLUTIONIST III

How much longer will a part of humankind accept the Mosaic Law of Moses, and his wizard-like brother, Aaron? This law of lies, as always, hides behind a veil of a god that they produced to fear. Most questions are answered with, "if you don't believe, and have no faith, you will burn in hell".

Most of all, if any person will read their myths with an open mind which is capable of accepting reality, it is easy to understand that the many great prophets of their time were against the wishes of the Mosaic Law and their followers.

Like Isaiah asked, "Pound your weapons into plow shears and war no more, and when you pray, pray in the closet, not on the corner for all to see".

THE EVOLUTIONIST III

There is no other answer than evolution for our being as we are. The unanswered still lies hidden concerning our future and our past. What has been will always be. Can this hold true with our future?

THE EVOLUTIONIST III

It's taken billions of what we call years to get to where we are today, with very little rest. You might consider this as "tough hoeing".

THE EVOLUTIONIST III

𝕳 ave you ever heard the expression, or have had some one tell you they can read your mind? This happens more often to a person who is inclined to tell a few lies. At some time or another, probably everyone has heard these words. Reading another's mind is occupational with some people. There are others who are just able to do it. When we were without a spoken language, it was a necessity to be able to read some other person's mind. When we had no eyes and lived in a cellular civilization, we had to converse in darkness, and I am sure that it was possible. There has always been a means of communication since our beginning, and will always be in our future.

Brain still has this ability. Brain lives, or exists, in the make up of every individual, yet it is still only brain. Each being of creation has a part of brain. Brain, which has as its base medulla/marrow, are not single brains. Brain is brain, no matter what it lives in. All brain is the makeup of one. All brain is in contact with itself. Perhaps not audible, but brain has a soundless connection within itself in the body of another.

When I refer to medulla/marrow, I have so far been unable to locate what it is that makes these two be the same, and also what they are made up of. There are still many things hidden from "brain", that will be understood in the future. I have found out a few things, though. Oblongata is a word that is used now in conjunction with medulla. Oblongated marrow in the past tense means,

THE EVOLUTIONIST III

prolonged. Medulla Oblongata is defined as the hindmost segment of brain. If the fore part of the brain is near the eyes, or in the forehead, and the medulla is the hindmost part of brain, then if the medulla is connected to the spinal cord, the medulla had to be first in brain construction. This is sort of like Darwin's, <u>The Descent of Man</u>, the dictionary explains - descent; the action of descending, going or coming down, downward motion. I always thought we were, or are, going up the ladder of evolution, or climbing out of the cave. "The Ascent of Man" would have described the happenings much better. Ascent, as the dictionary explains, "to comply with a desire, as influenced by ones senses, the concurrence of the will, compliance with a desire". Up seems to have more desire than down.

THE EVOLUTIONIST III

How stupid could I be? I am observing all life as I live it, and yet I have spent less time observing myself, and the physical changes this body, I refer to as me, has made.

Why should my hair change from blond as a child, to near-black as a teenager, to gray in my fifties, and to near-white in my seventies? Why should my teeth be replaced at the end of of my childhood with permanent teeth? Why should wisdom teeth force their way in, behind my regular molars, only to be chiseled out because there wasn't enough room for them, while my lungs were digesting laughing gas, or ether?

Why is it that, at around twelve years old, my breasts began to swell, as a woman's, and then, a year later, they were back to normal. Certain foods, when I was a youngster, made me gag. There were many other of these drastic problems, but today, they are all gone; replaced by some which seem worse, and yet I live with them, and have finally learned to keep most of them to myself, until now.

THE EVOLUTIONIST III

Haeckel, in his <u>History of Creation, Vol. II</u>, states, "In its inseparable connection with the body, the human soul or mind . . ." In other words, the soul and mind are considered to be the same, or one, to Haeckel

I'm sure, as we become more enlightened to the facts of life, we are going to understand that there is much more to becoming one with creation than just the soul and mind.

THE EVOLUTIONIST III

Different levels? Perhaps our intelligence is brighter than another. However, the one with less intelligence, naturally, requires less to Be.

THE EVOLUTIONIST III

It's time we stopped taking things for granted. It could happen any day!

THE EVOLUTIONIST III

To build a fire, and then beat on logs with rocks or sticks, and then have leaders, and followers, who commence jumping up and down over and over in a rhythmic order, and circle the fire while jumping or stomping their feet and chanting, could be the simplest form of mass hypnosis. As the rhythm of the beat becomes more intense, the hypnosis spreads to the audience, and the total minds become as one when the leaders scream, and everything ceases and silence takes over.

For the orgasm to be "real", it had to start easy, build up into ecstasy, and then abruptly end. To start at a slow pace, build up, and then slow to the pace at which it started, could not produce the effect of the sudden stop. This can be compared to eating a meal. To take the meal away when the satisfaction of eating it is the highest, makes the desire for more even greater.

For incantations such as this dance around the fire to spread, the slow rhythm starts it off, then it builds to a frenzy, and then suddenly stops as the mind's orgasm completes, and all is silent to let brain digest what has taken place. It is simple to see that fire is the real foundation for the spell. Then to beat a rhythm would make it much stronger, and then to dance and chant around the fire is the ultimate, or climax.

This is a simple thing that still works today, and was not spread from tribe to tribe. True, it could have spread slightly, but the majority of this type of religious service was invented by small,

THE EVOLUTIONIST III

tribal families. Each had this ritual begin in a simple fashion, and then the customs began, and slowly the witch doctor moved on the scene. Today they call him a preacher.

THE EVOLUTIONIST III

There are many leads in our research concerning the background of humankind. Let those who feel they are here for a purpose join hands with those who search to understand through what, and how, we acquired the position in which we now stand.

Fossils are the foundation of the physical sciences. It seems sensory is the spirit through what we know as God. It is possible that God could be the producer of both.

Sensory seems to dwell in the body of being. That is, the spirit exists by existing in all, yet unseen. Necessities for existence of the physical must be furnished by the body itself. To exist, one must acquire, through digestion, as much food as daily energy requires.

This does not exclude all of the "other" physical bodies, both seen and unseen, who also require so much food for their requirement of being. The spirit exists through all of our physical bodies. The seen or unseen possibly require no food, only a body to exist in.

A tree searches the sky for the rays of the sun, just as the plant. Yet existence is also furnished these sessile bodies through the food of the earth.

God speaks through all. It's up to all creation to furnish food for energy, so that God may continue to exist: Through Us!

THE EVOLUTIONIST III

Our bodies have developed much better than any caveman could have hoped for, and nature was still only nature. This was the time of Carl Jung, one hundred or so years after Darwin was born. Evolution was just beginning to stick its tongue out at us. The Spirit was praying to get a few more years out of life. A problem, at that time, was not, "Will I be able to catch a deer for dinner tonight?, but, "Will I be able to pay the rent?". The asylums were filled with poor souls who had gone mad for lack of being able to fulfill the requirements of Christianity. And the Pope was blessing cannon balls.

THE EVOLUTIONIST III

Evidently, they are happy being "that way", or there would not be a way to be "that way". After all, there have always been those who have been happy being "that way".

THE EVOLUTIONIST III

If the God of Israel worked six days, and then rested on the seventh, and everything was "good", like He said; whose kidding who?

THE EVOLUTIONIST III

Membrane is a fine skin, or a thin, soft, pliable sheet or layer, especially of animal or vegetable tissue, serving as a covering, or lining, as for an organ, a part of either plant or animal membrane. Take heed of this, of either plant or animal.

Blood, whom most people see as a red fluid, and describe as something that circulates through the heart, arteries, and veins of animals, is also described as the sap, or fluid, of a plant. So we could describe the blood of an animal, or the juice or sap of a plant, as both being circulatory liquid.

A plasma membrane is a very thin membrane surrounding the cytoplasm of a plant or animal cell. Cytoplasm is the protoplasm of a cell, outside of the nucleus of this cell.

Cell, in the study of biology, is a very small, complex unit of protoplasm, usually with a nucleus, cytoplasm, and enclosing membrane. All plants and animals are made up of one or more cells that usually combine to form various tissues.

Tissues as taught, in the study of biology, as the substance of an organic body, or organ, consisting of cells and intercellular material, or any of the distinct, structural materials of an organism, having a particular function in either plants or animals.

I have written about pith in other papers, and its relationship to bone marrow. Pith is the soft core of plant stems, and makes up the means for sap to circulate. In the disguise of marrow, it does the same thing in bones. Also, pith in the stems of a sort of bamboo

THE EVOLUTIONIST III

seems to be one of the main sources of food energy for gorillas and perhaps pandas.

In this paper I am attempting to show or explain the kinship of plants to animals. Today, humankind are beginning to construct a foundation for the belief of their relationship to <u>other</u> animals. After all, it is now accepted by most, through the educational study of biology, that we are an animal. Not a different kind of animal with a different kind of brain, but an animal containing the same molecular make up of all animals. Only our physical shapes differ.

In the near future, probably the twenty-first century, I am sure our relationship to the "other" animals will be fully accepted. With this acceptance to understand the fact, or theory now, that we are also in full relationship with the plants, will then follow.

Then will come the time, as it did a few years ago, that we will truly have pet rocks.

THE EVOLUTIONIST III

I always thought that the brand of jeans called Levi were named after the Levites. The Levites, according to the Old Testament, were a tribe of Israel that traced their descent back to Levi. Levi was the third son of Jacob, by Leah, and was the High Priest of Israel.

Today, I read about Leviathan. Leviathan, in Jewish mythology, was a creature that became ruler of the seas, and threatened the world. Leviathan was later killed, and they preserved his body by salting it down, and used it to feed the people.

Levi-athan seems to make more sense when it comes to naming the toughest jeans in the world.

THE EVOLUTIONIST III

Near our beginning it could have been possible that what we call our bodies had no opening, such as a mouth or an anus. They say we fed ourselves through the method of saturation from the outside elements. After digesting these components, the secretion seeped out of our bodies. Saturation and permeation had to be our method of receiving food for energy and excreting waste..

In reality, the less parts any type of machinery requires, the less problems it has.

THE EVOLUTIONIST III

I don't feel that beings attached to another by sight can align themselves with being mentally connected. Understanding is a gift for eternity.

THE EVOLUTIONIST III

The question is in us. The answer is in the atmosphere.

THE EVOLUTIONIST III

The earth is spinning to the east and the mountains in the west are casting shadows on the eastern ridges. All at once a jet plane zooms across the sky, and has no respect for either. It's on a mission of speed that out speeds the earth, which has been fastest since the beginning of time. And as I write this paper, a spider, yellow-gold in color and about the size of a pin head, crawls across the paper, with no regard for the jet, or the earth, or that I'm writing this paper about him. He's lucky as hell I'm not a lizard or a frog in the mood for a spider dinner.

Anyway, when I was a boy, like everyone else, we had cats and dogs as pets. I can remember going to the market and asking the butcher for liver for the cat and a bone for the dog. They used to give those away. Many times my mother fried the liver and from the bone made soup for the family - my brother, Gerry, and me. But again, a lot, or at least half of the time, the cat got the liver and the dog got the bone.

The real purpose of this paper is to enlighten others to the fact that cats no longer get liver, they get crunchy cat food similar to our Grape Nuts, and the big, ferocious dog settles for Purina Dog Chow, and loves it.

And while these two are feasting (I've got to stop here for a minute. I never realized how close these two words were spelled, and that mean the exact opposite - fasting and feasting). Anyway, the diet seems to have changed before the evolutionary changes

THE EVOLUTIONIST III

came. I never dreamt I would watch dogs and cats eat anything but meat. What made me put this on paper were the birds that visit my lawn daily here at Kernville, California (really, it's Old Kernville, or "Whiskey Flats". The lake has covered Old Kernville and they had to move it a few miles up to the mouth of the river.) These birds don't come for Hansel and Gretel bread crumbs, they're after what lives in the grass and shrubbery around the house, and are in direct competition with the lizards, who crouch in front and crawl the walls for their bug meals. Every once in a while, a prehistoric bird called a road runner will walk past with a lizard in its mouth, just getting even for the bugs.

It's really different when you grow older, I always visualized a bird eating seeds. I guess that only happens with canaries. No wonder they sing, the rest are eating bugs. I have the feeling that Jesus and John the Baptist ate a lot of locust "bugs" when they were hustling around the deserts.

It's nice how things change with time and age. I used to think Santa Claus was God's brother.

THE EVOLUTIONIST III

𝔐y own life has taught me this. On the twenty-first of December, 1999, I will have spent 76 years on this planet earth with you. For these 76 years I have existed with you, I have been forced, as much as possible, to live by the rules of morality. Your laws have worried me by their coming and going, and some times the penalties have been uncontrollable. Too harsh at times, and too lenient at times; however, a necessity. In my time, there have been many laws made and many laws changed. A law in Wyoming, that could possibly still be in effect, states that you're not allowed to eat anything, including pretzels, in a bar. On the other hand, California has a law which makes a bar serve food.
    You've really got to watch out when your traveling.

THE EVOLUTIONIST III

We live surrounded by what we feel to be others. These others have physical shapes of all sorts, some like us, some like others. Yet with all of these others, it's hard to believe that we are other than ourselves. We live within life. We have our physical shapes to prove it. Mentality has been created by our observations, and passed on through the regeneration of life. When we finally reach the point of fully understanding, no matter how many of these generations we pass through, peace and relaxation will be ours.

THE EVOLUTIONIST III

Have we descended, or ascended? Darwin, bless him, gave his book the title, <u>The Descent of Man</u>. In which direction are we really headed? Descending, or ascending?

THE EVOLUTIONIST III

Once we get another solution, we'll have another religion. I guess that will be all right, just as long as someone doesn't try to run it.

THE EVOLUTIONIST III

Reason is man's highest gift, the only prerogative that essentially distinguishes him from the lower animals. This statement has been issued over and over by worldly scientists, and is truly false. The basic brain is in all creation. The basic life is in all creation. The basic thoughts are in all creation. The basic questions are in all creation, the basic dreams are in all creation. In other words, basics are a part of all. Reason seems to be continually used as a means to explain humankind as superior, which is not true.

By reason only can we attain a correct knowledge of the world and a solution towards its great problems. It is by reason that we arrive in the jungle of doubt that we are existing in. Reason has presented creation with problems more than solutions. An example would be that because a person sees the turn signal of the car in front of him flashing a right turn, the automobile will definitely turn right. This is a gross understatement. There are many reasons that the signal may not be true, and I'm sure that readers of this paper are well aware of what they are. Reasoning is always a choice. Yes and no tests are a perfect example. You are required to reason. There is no single answer to any question; our attorneys are proving this today by the way they mentally construe or misconstrue our laws.

Reasoning is a method of summarizing. It is truly a means of breaking down a situation or problem, in order to reach what the

THE EVOLUTIONIST III

mind feels is the best answer for a particular situation. All creation has to have this ability in order to exist, and evolve.

A case in mind could be any small animal, including humankind, attempting to cross the highway. First of all, reasoning that something many times larger than you can hurt you, is a simple answer to that problem. If any four legged animal, big or small, did not have the power to reason, it would merely walk across the road without caring. Maybe they did about seventy years ago, and so did humans. Neither walks in front of a car now. They either run or wait for the car to pass. In fact, the four legged creatures are smarter at waiting than the bipeds in clothes. Humankind will stand next to road and wait for the car to pass, risking the driver losing control and hitting them, but the four legged animal will usually run off, where they are sure to be safe while the car passes, and then cross the road.

I could go on and on with comparisons concerning the question of humans and the other animals, and how both have the power of reasoning. Einstein had a simple solution for this, "If you have a good thought or idea, and you want to get rid of it, tell it to someone who has a closed mind."

THE EVOLUTIONIST III

Why is it that when I look to the north I feel that I am looking up? The mountains to the north are no higher than the mountains to the south. Why is it that when I drive to the north I feel I am driving up hill? And when I drive to the south I feel as though I'm driving down hill. When I drive to the east or west I feel that I am driving level, and as I drive west some times I feel like I am standing still and the earth is revolving under me, which it really is, only a lot faster than I am driving. Yet when I stand still I have no feeling of movement yet my body is resting on a globe that is spinning over five hundred miles an hour, and much faster as it speeds around the sun, and God only knows how fast the sun is traveling as we orbit it, and the sun is sailing along on its galactic orbit.

With all of this taking place why should we worry? After all, where have we been, and where are we going? Or is it just going to be orbit after orbit from now on?

THE EVOLUTIONIST III

We take life, more or less for granted. In reality, we are traveling on our planet Earth at speeds unthought of through the universe, on a trip we can not realize. Many still feel we are standing still.

It will be impossible for even the healthiest in the physical and mental shape of today to travel at the speeds which will be required in the future.

As the planes circle our earth today, at over twice the speed that the earth revolves, rockets in the future will travel unseen, through an atmosphere we call universal space.

THE EVOLUTIONIST III

If I make it easy for you, and you're making it easy for me, all we both have to do is put forth a little effort.

If I make it tough for you, and you're making it tough for me, then we're both busy all of the time.

THE EVOLUTIONIST III

Those who live in rocks must go with the weather, until the weather sets them free.

THE EVOLUTIONIST III

𝕀 am certain that I have driven well over a million miles in my life. It took a lot of cars, and a lot of time to do this. During this time, I have spent a lot of time behind the wheel thinking about many different things. One of these was the roads that I have traveled on. These freeways, highways, and roads were constructed of all sorts of materials, but made up mainly of oil, sand, and gravel. However, this was not the way they were in the beginning. The beginnings of almost all of our roads have been trails. First for the quadrupeds, then bipeds, then wagons with teams, and finally the automobile. And lets not forget the bicycle or the motorcycle.

As I traveled along from the Pacific to the Atlantic and from Mexico City to Fairbanks, Alaska, I often thought about how all of these roads came to be. It's very easy to see what has taken place in most cases. Most roads follow rivers. The reason being water to exist on. After all to travel thirty miles a day walking, or on horseback, is quite a long ways.

This evening, while riding up the Kern River, I got a glimpse of how the road up this canyon really came to be. In a few places, the small shale rocks are still piled on the side of steep cliffs, where the Indians had placed them to make the trip easier. The canyon up the Kern is spectacular. Almost solid rock, as I'm sure it was when its formation first took place, it is now sparsely covered with crumbled rock and sand amongst the large boulders. Some are twenty feet in diameter and others, in their original positions, are

THE EVOLUTIONIST III

thousands of feet thick.

Tiny rodents were possibly the first trail makers up the canyon, with coyotes, bobcats, lions, deer, and bears making the trail wider and wider. The Indian tribes that live here in the Kern River Valley were probably the first to actually do any construction on the trail, and this was clearing brush and placing shale in the bad places, for footing.

As the settlers came into the valley and began raising cattle, the desire to travel the canyon became a reality. First, teams and wagons wore the road wider and wider. The extension of the road grew longer and clearing brush turned into setting off dynamite to blast the rock cliffs for a future road that wagons could travel. Bridges were constructed out of the trees, and the road continued up the river.

Today the road travels high up into the Sierra Mountains and is only closed in the snowy winter months. Asphalt pavement covers the rocks and gravel where the animals had first traveled, and automobiles loaded with family vacationers ride where the Indians first walked.

Almost any road you travel on today has the same history as this Kern River Road. Although larger tractors have now made it possible to take shortcuts through mountains, which were impossible less than fifty years ago, and what used to take months to do can be accomplished in days.

THE EVOLUTIONIST III

When you come onto something that you feel is good, the first thing you should do is share it with another. Watch their reaction. If you feel they have accepted it as good, then continue to display it. Eventually it will spread to all: this good, which at first was only known to you is now an advantage to all, and will be held sacred by all. This good, which you discovered, is now a part of you for the future of others.

This was my first recognition of comprehending a way of my always being a part of life. Every existence of nature at one time or another, discovers, or perhaps stumbles across one or so of these valuable things, or situations. They did not only come to us by the prophets or scientists, but by the simplest of God's creatures. I'm sure that if we never saw anything fly, we would not have had the urge to fly.

My first enlightenment of grasping a thought which I could use to attach myself to eternity was this simple explanation. I tried in every way possible since this discovery to expound these words into a simple way of explaining our possession of eternity. The more I read and studied nature, the more I could see this process was growing larger and larger in my mind and spirit. Until I read this same line of thought in the novel, "The Education of Little Tree", I thought it was only my personal idea, but I was really glad to see that someone else had this same thought. Now I can, even more, understand how this thought is true, and how it would be

THE EVOLUTIONIST III

impossible for any of creation to live without discovering something, big or small that would be a benefit to life.

THE EVOLUTIONIST III

Hi Bill -

I've been thinkin'.

Most people go to church because they feel there's only two places to go, when it's over, heaven or hell, and they don't want to take a chance, and not be able to get in the first one. Sometimes where they've been or where they are worries them too.

Evolution requires understanding, basically requiring time which most people would rather spend at the beach, or in the mountains, or sneaking in the rear door of the local tavern.

Faith, is much easier.

Tom

THE EVOLUTIONIST III

When herds of cattle gather in the winter in extreme cold weather, they alternate from the center of the herd to the outside of the herd. In this manner, everyone keeps warm, most of the time. I wonder if the same holds true for the tiny micro-organisms that live on the rocks?

Lungs are stomachs for certain foods that the atmosphere contains, along with oxygen.

THE EVOLUTIONIST III

For several days I have been concentrating on the functions of brain. Medulla, thalamus and ganglia seem to hound my thinking. These three, in my opinion, seem to be the basic, or beginning, parts which make up brain.

Le Conte states, "We may find for example, a right-hand rotation of atoms is associated with love, and a left handed rotation is associated with hate." Also, brain cells, he feels, can be agitated, and thought begins. Stimulation of brain seems to come from these agitations just as Aladdin's lamp reacted when it was rubbed. Thought and desire are both the results of brain stimulation, and perhaps good thoughts could be the result of atoms spinning to the right, and bad thoughts are the results of atoms spinning to the left. I wonder if this same thing holds true concerning whether a person is a male or female, or left or right handed.

It could be possible that to become was first a desire of the spirit, and medulla was created from some simple agitated desire. Medulla being that which furnishes breath and circulation to our physical being, or the cell of the beginning. The urge to Be comes from many directions; however, to Be, there must be a beginning. This beginning has steadily forced its way through the essence of life.

To understand to be alive required, or requires, tangible evidence. What other force for understanding could comprehend life than brain, which dwells in all creation. Eyes see, hands feel, feet

THE EVOLUTIONIST III

walk, ears hear, mouths eat and talk, and noses breathe; only brain gives directional life, power; Being!

Medulla seems to be the beginning of this source of power. There are those who say medulla was, in the beginning, the result of a swelling on the tip of the spinal cord or nerve ending. This could possibly be. However, my feelings are medulla was the organ that created the spinal cord, and us. It is a blatant fact that medulla was first, and medulla / marrow seem to be the same, and also, that both medulla and marrow are brain power behind both plant and animal life. Medulla / marrow was our beginning, and the spinal cord in animal life and the stem of the plant were their creation.

For billions of years, in other words, an inconceivable amount of time, or since the beginning of brain and then with the development of the body, humankind have suffered with pain at the base of the skull, where medulla lives as a part of brain. In other words, the medulla makes the connection with the spinal cord at this location. As medulla sensed a need for additional organs for the body, the body expanded under the directions of brain, medulla / marrow. The more parts to function on the body, the more brain was required to operate these new organs.

Returning to the pain, or burning sensation, that comes and goes at the base of the skull, or the peak of the neck, it is here that medulla exists. Could it be that when brain gets fed too many thoughts, or problems, or perhaps non-directional understanding, that this burning results, and the pain from the body desires to make it impossible for more thoughts to be fed through the medulla, or the medulla has shut off body desires to the rest of brain as the pain gets worse. Again perhaps medulla understands that what the physical body desires, or is asking for, can not now be supplied. In other words medulla is telling the body to rest, or simply calm down and relax for a while by cutting short the breathing and circulation. It is not only telling the body to do this, but by having the power to slow the breathing and circulation, it is forcing the body to sit or lay down.

Soon these pains are relieved and the body is once again slowly returning to normal reactions, and the pain is gone, and the body has learned something new! Take it easy.

THE EVOLUTIONIST III

Close calls come to everyone, and each may consider themselves, "lucky to be alive".

One instance in my own life, I was working at my desk at Willow Spring International Raceway, in Rosamond, California. Neicie Kelly, my secretary, was sitting right across from me, at her desk. There was about ten feet between us. It was a summer day, and a lightning storm was happening. Suddenly, a bolt of lightning struck very close to the office. An instant later a loud bang lit up the office and a ball of fire about ten inches in diameter flashed into existence on top of a filing cabinet, which was against the wall, between both of us.

This episode only took seconds, but rattled us both pretty good. When it was over, I looked at the microphone which was setting on the metal cabinet and it had been welded to the cabinet. We went outside and could see where the lightning had struck a speaker pole, which was a telephone pole we were then using as speaker poles. The pole was split wide open for about ten foot, down from the top. The speaker was okay. The lightning had traveled down the pole on the speaker wire, about three hundred feet and into the office. To both Neicie and I, this seemed to be a very close call, at least one that I know will never happen again, in the same way. The next week was spent installing all new four by four metal poles, and the old telephone poles were gone. By this happening, I had learned to put ground wires on everything.

THE EVOLUTIONIST III

This seems to be much more than a coincidence, but animals and plants have a thing described, in both cases, as hair. This could be another "thing" showing the relationship of animals to plants. Brain seems to exist in the plants as pith, and in the animals as medulla.

I wonder what we will discover next to further this relationship between plants and animals. Soon, the vegetarian humanists will shrink to nothing in their attempt not to "kill", to be able to eat.

THE EVOLUTIONIST III

All things are nonexistent when it comes to sensations, thought, memory, or imagination, except brain. You can blame that on your mind, a conception of brain.

THE EVOLUTIONIST III

When eye contact is made with another there is no need for language. A nod or a smile is enough.

THE EVOLUTIONIST III

One afternoon, while we had no paid hunting parties, my son Chris and I decided to go over to the Grasshopper, about fifty miles west of Wisdom, Montana, and hunt some deer for a part of our winter meat. My wife, Maxine, got the food ready for the camp, and we hooked the army jeep behind our old school bus, which we used as a portable hunting camp. We loaded things up, called the dogs, and the six of us, three people and three dogs, took off for the hunt.

The three dogs consisted of Wing, a small cocker spaniel and poodle mix, Flossy, a glass-eyed Australian sheep dog, and Rocky, a black pomeranian. They were not hunting dogs, just friends.

The school bus had a wood stove and three cots, and just the bare necessities for a hunting camp. The only bad thing about it, if you had a fire going in the cook stove while you were traveling, you had to watch that no hay trucks were following you. The sparks might burn them down.

It took us a couple of hours to get over Carol Hill and up Dice Creek, where we stopped and set up camp. About four the next morning, we got up and had breakfast. After we had eaten, Chris and I got our rifles and got in the Jeep. I called out to Maxine and told her not to let the dogs out or they'd follow us. Wing was the worst, he loved to chase the deer.

We took off. There was some snow on the ground in

places, and, as we followed the creek up the canyon, there was snow everywhere, and it was fresh. This was going to be an easy hunt. We branched off on different roads two or three times, and drove through the creek a couple of times. There were lots of deer tracks crossing the road.

After about five miles, I stopped the Jeep, and we got out. Chris went up the road to the left, towards the ridge, and I took the trail up the canyon towards Baldy Mountain. We were up near the head of Dice Creek. I had walked along the trail about two miles, and was resting on a log in front of an old mining shack.

All at once, I heard a noise, and then I heard something panting or breathing hard. I didn't figure on it being a deer because there had been no shots, and what other reason would a deer have to run and get that tired? Then I saw that it was Wing. He had escaped the bus. Not only him, but I knew exactly what had happened as Flossy and Rocky came in sight. They were all smiling and wagging their tails. What else could I do than say "Hi"? That took care of the morning hunt for me.

I called the dogs, and we headed back to the Jeep. I thought about what had happened, and cussed all of them out. We made our way down the canyon, and they stayed behind me about a hundred feet, for fear I would really get mad and throw a rock at them.

When I got to the jeep, I could see their tracks, and I knew Wing was the gang leader. His tracks didn't even falter about whose tracks to follow, mine or Chris', when they got to the Jeep. I got

THE EVOLUTIONIST III

them in the Jeep and we headed back to the camp. At each junction, I checked Wing's tracks to see if he had any trouble following the Jeep. He never even slowed down. He had followed the tracks of the Jeep just like they were my tracks. I had often wondered about his ability to follow tire tracks.

On another time, my wife and I were out for a Sunday ride down the road that followed the Big Hole River. About three miles past Johnson Corner, a local bar, a bunch of deer ran across the road. Wing saw them, so I let him out of the car and away he went, yapping as he ran up the mountain after the deer. Maxine and I watched as he went out of sight. I started the car and turned around and we went back to Johnson's Corner for a beer.

Johnson was tending bar, and he asked where we had been. He saw us go by earlier. I told him we had seen some deer down the road and that we had let Wing out to chase them for awhile. He asked, "How far down the road?". "About three miles," I answered. He handed us the beer with the lids on them, and I told him we would drink them at the bar while we waited for the dog.

Johnson looked at us kind of funny, and asked, "How the hell is the dog going to know where you are?" I told him he could smell the tires.

Sure as hell, after about two hours, here came Wing with his tongue hanging out and panting.

This one's kind of funny. It was about thirty below zero, and I let him out of the house to chase a mink that had run across the road in front. He ran out the door and was right after the mink. About a half hour later, I heard him scratching on the door. I opened it up and there he was, steaming in the zero weather. The icicles were around his mouth, and he could not open it because the fur had frozen together. He walked right over and sat next to the wood heat stove, with his mouth right next to it. He worked his jaws around until the heat finally melted the snow, and he could break the icy fur loose, and open his mouth. He stretched it open to make sure every thing was working okay, looked at me and smiled, and then walked over to the window to see if anything else was happening out front.

Back to the deer hunt. Chris got one that morning, and we went back later for another one. We took no dogs the second time.

THE EVOLUTIONIST III

𝔄 beaver didn't just pop into existence building dams everywhere. Nor did birds just get born building nests. Just as man, these accomplishments took millions of years.

Bank beavers, in the Centennial Valley of southwestern Montana, dig long tunnels in the earth, through which they travel from pond to pond, and house to house. At intervals, there are vertical tunnels, which are used as opening for emergencies. They have houses that are just the same as others, but these tunnels serve a more useful means of travel than the thick ice of winter. One thing they have and still use, which is comparable to man five thousand years ago, is a dung pile. Perhaps a little cleaner, though, the beaver pats a little mud over the dung each time they use the pile. I've never read in the history of mankind where man took the time to pat mud over the dung when they finished a bowel movement. Even a cat does better than man; they bury it!

Birds also spent millions of years in the development of their nests, and there seem to be almost as many nest designs as there are bird species.

The real purpose of this paper is to make humankind aware of the fact that we are no more a chosen thing to be, than a flea. All natural things happen to all natural beings. The one funny thing about it is that mankind actually feel, and are taught, that they are so much better off than the rest of creation. I don't know how they can feel this way. I never see the dog or horse paying the hospital for curing the "man".

THE EVOLUTIONIST III

How come "p" looks like, or faces one way, and "q" looks just like "p", but faces the other way. And besides this, both are right next to each other in the alphabet.

Then look at the letter "V". It really doesn't seem that whoever was making up the English alphabet was sincere about what they were doing. To make a "w" they just put two "v's" together. Come to think about it, they're right next to each other in the alphabet also.

THE EVOLUTIONIST III

It seems that when generation took place, a few million years ago, it was a matter of splitting ourselves, to become two beings. I understand that this same process is still taking place. I wonder if humankind will ever return to that method? It seems that it would be easier, but probably not as much fun.

THE EVOLUTIONIST III

Humankind should not worry about each other, but should think about the things they create that bring worry.

THE EVOLUTIONIST III

James Trefil wrote the following statement in the opening of the final chapter of his book, <u>Are we Unique?</u>:

> Let me begin by reafirming my belief that the brain is nothing more than a physical system. It may be a highly complicated system, one that involves both electrical and chemical methods of communication. It may be interconnected like nothing else in the universe, but at bottom it is still a system made of atoms and molecules.
>
> There is no need to postulate the existence of anything like a soul or any special kind of mystical experience to understand the brain or consciousness.

In my opinion, it is true that brain is a physical organ made up of atoms and molecules. However, each of these atoms and molecules also contain what we might consider brain. To have intelligence and consciousness, one must have a receptor. The closest I have come to qualify a thing as the receptor is brain. The actual size of brain has never been determined. In my mind, I can not determine a size that fits brain. This is much like time and space. It takes only one of anything, be it atom or molecule, to contain intelligance, and consciousness. When "ones" get together they climb into a cell, their house, or temple. These cells form a village and become an organ. Organs form bodies and bodies get their orders through brain.

THE EVOLUTIONIST III

Trying to put a number on how many of anything there is in life, for now, I would say to be impossible. However, we seem to be putting all of our effort in the opposite direction. It is the small "things" in life that are the easiet to handle, and understand. Right now we are struggling to understand the makeup of the atom. It is generally held to consist of a positively charged nucleus, in which is concentrated most of the mass of the atom, and around which orbit negatively charged electrons.

To postulate, or assume the atom to be true, is no longer neccessery. Through the firing of the atomic bomb, we need no more proof. By this you can fully understand that the scientific world is not groping in darkness. It is this same science that is bringing peace to our world. To postulate a thought may pass it into a stage of aphorismic wisdom. This aphorism can then be transferred on to be an axiom: Universally-conceded principle; a maxim, rule, law.

However, law brings on law. Thought brings on thought. The drop brought on the molecule, the molecule brought on the cell, the cell brought on the atom, the atom brought on ???. Soon, through this same process, the question mark will disappear.

To say brain is a highly complicated system of communication is a gross understatement of what brain really is. Brain is an automatic means of communication. Brain is automatic in the highest sense of the word. Without brain, the universal nervous system would collapse. Yet brain is where we are settled at

THE EVOLUTIONIST III

the present time. Just as science is aspiring to understand the atom, at the same time the connection of brain, mind, and consciousness are being scrutinized.

    I continually pester brain for the answer to the makeup of medulla, which by now you must know is the basic makeup of brain. Perhaps medulla goes even further than that. If medulla and marrow are the same, as some say, I have seen marrow. In fact, I like the taste of marrow. Medulla is in brain, but brain is a little salty, I have only tasted brain one time. Pith, which is the core of plant-life stems, is being continually eaten by the gorrilas. I love the pith on the inside of the peeling of navel oranges. By the way, if you take a piece of orange peel and fold it over so the outside is folded in and light a match and squeeze it over the flame, the flame will flare up.

    I wonder if that's medulla?
    So long!

THE EVOLUTIONIST III

When I was about eight years old, I seemed to have a sore throat much of the time. This sore throat finally developed into streptococcus infection, commonly referred to as a strep throat, and put me on the edge of death for about two weeks. The doctor, who in those times came to the house, told my mother I would have to get well before they could remove my tonsils. There were no antibiotics at that time, "Just give him orange juice and pineapple juice to drink", were the doctors orders. "Let me know when Billy gets well, and we'll take those bad tonsils out."

After a couple of weeks I got well, and the appointment was set for me to get my tonsils out. I got up that morning, walked about a quarter of a mile to the hospital, went in, laid down on the operating table, they gave me ether, and I passed out. I don't know how long it took, but several hours later I came to, and they asked me how I felt. I could hardly speak, but I got out a squeaky, "okay".

Just like that, they said, "Okay, you can go home". I got up, walked out of the room and into the hall. "Tell your mother it was pretty serious. Your tonsils had to be taken out with a spoon, they were so bad. Also tell her that she can bring the twenty dollars in for the operation when she's got the money. Good bye." I nodded, yes, and walked out the front door, and back to my house. Life was a lot simpler in those days, and a heck of a lot cheaper.

THE EVOLUTIONIST III

𝕋 homas Hobbes, an English political philosopher (1588-1679), wrote the book <u>Leviathan</u> in 1651, at the age of 63. Leviathan, in Jewish mythology, was a creature that became the ruler of the seas. Legend relates on the 5th day of creation a male and female Leviathan were created. To prevent the destruction of earth, the female was slain immediately and its flesh was preserved with salt to provide food for the righteous in the world to come.

THE EVOLUTIONIST III

Evolutionary thought does not contain mystic dogma. Evolutionary teachings present an explanation of eternal life, as it truly is. Eternity belongs to all creation. Lack of understanding is the only problem.

THE EVOLUTIONIST III

𝕰at, or ate. Three letters, that when re-adjusted, change from present tense to past tense.

THE EVOLUTIONIST III

How is it that evolutionistic scientists could pass over one of the most outstanding, natural observations of our present and past physical history?

In my research over the past forty-six years, I have never seen the subject of this paper mentioned. I have read many times of our beginning taking place in Africa. I have observed for years and read the words of the greatest scientists. Biblical history has mentioned them only as barbarians, and stated no more.

I am speaking of the "Orange race", the "red-heads", "The Vikings". These were the conquerors of the British Isles, a species of humankind that I personally place in the position of being sired by ancestors which could have a history older than any others on this planet.

In the species of ants, we have black ants, red ants, and white ants. Black could be associated with brown and red, and white could be associated with brown and red, and red could be associated with both brown and black. Red at night becomes black, and black at night is black, and sometimes very dark blue in daylight. White skin becomes browned by summer, and returns to white in winter. Orange becomes more red in winter and orange in the summer. However, an Orange haired person has orangeish-white skin.

Our north and south poles were the first to cool off on the planet earth. The reason being that the axis of the earth let these two

THE EVOLUTIONIST III

poles go into darkness alternately, while the equator was in the sunlight at all time, except at night, when it was on the opposite side of the sun. Tropical forests covered these two poles first, which is natural. The forests then proceeded to grow, or extend towards the equator.

Today, most of the vegetables that grow around the arctic circle are three or four times larger than those grown in the United States. The shell fish are also much larger. Then, too, the humankind from that area seem to me to be taller than usual. Not only did they have orange hair, but the Norsemen were feared by all other races in our early history.

The Orange-men have never been considered a race in themselves, and I feel it is time, before we are all stewed together, that we should give them recognition, and make a deeper study of their history. After all, they are the only species of humankind mentioned in any dictionaries, until recently.

I began this study while checking different information concerning orangutans, and the reason for their having orange colored hair. I have the feeling that their origination could have been from this same area of the far north, when it was infested with tropical forests.

THE EVOLUTIONIST III

As the anthropologists and paleontologists search for the fossils of our past history, they often come across heaps of biped skulls, usually in caves. These skulls have been cracked open, and brain has been extracted. It is the belief that those who cracked the skull open ate the contents, brain. There could have been several reasons for this. My belief is that the taste of brain is very salty, and those who ate the brain were, in reality, after the salt taste. Many think that they may have been eating brain to get the advantage of the others' spirit. It's hard to believe that they knew anything about spirit then. After all, they made woman a god because they never understood what caused her to have children.

If you want to know for sure how salty brain tastes and you can't stand the thought of eating brain, the next time your sinus is dripping from your nose, taste it with the tip of your tongue. That is, if you haven't already done it when you were a kid.

THE EVOLUTIONIST III

The beginning seems to be inconceivable. However, the life displayed by creation is undoubtable. Many of the creatures displayed before us, and who are very truthfully our brothers, are unable to see, yet their sensory power is used towards seeing, and allows them to exist. By this I mean, these molecular Beings, a part of us, live in a world of comparison to themselves, and yet this world is a part of our world. Size seems to be the problem, for us not recognizing them.

THE EVOLUTIONIST III

If we are physically related to plants, and we inhale oxygen, and we exhale carbon dioxide; and the plants inhale carbon dioxide and exhale oxygen, then medulla/marrow, which is contained as a basis of brain makeup, in both animal and plant, must thrive on both oxygen and carbon dioxide.

I wonder? Perhaps we might classify both to contain what Dr. Paul Kammerer coined in four very meaningful words, "The sap of life".

Soon, you'll be hearing and reading more from me concerning a self-taught biologist who physically existed from 1880 to 1926, and his feelings about how his evolutionistic happenings take place.

THE EVOLUTIONIST III

𝕰 volution = a physical connection with eternity.

THE EVOLUTIONIST III

It's a natural truth considering the size and make up of the cell. The smallest are unseen, yet they contain, or bring into existence, what we are. Conglomerations of these cells make up creation.

Below these cells, we have atomic structure, closer to the essence of life. And at the present, we are examining a "thing" called quark. A quark, in the <u>Oxford Dictionary</u> is, "Any of a group of sub-atomic particles (orig. three in number) conceived of as having a reactional electric charge, and making up, in different combinations, the hadrons, but not detected in the free state."

Hedron - First used in Russian, with the spelling "adron". Any strongly interacting subatomic particle. Hence hadronic. In 1962, L. B. Okun said, "In this report I shall call strongly interacting particles hadrons, and the corresponding decays hadronic". <u>NEW SCIENTIST</u>, May, 1966 - The particles, so-called baryons and mesons, collectively called hadrons.

Baryon - any hyperon other than the proton or neutron.

Meson - 1947, <u>SCIENTIFIC NEWS</u>, mesons are the most penetrating component of cosmic rays.

Cosmic Rays - High energy radiations with great penetrative power which are incident on the earth from all directions, and which originate in outer space (primary radiation) or are produced in the upper atmosphere by the primary radiation (secondary radiation). So cosmic radiation.

THE EVOLUTIONIST III

Evidently then, the meson is a component of cosmic rays, and the cosmic rays are a product of outer space. So, if we want to take our study further, we will have to go to outer space. Earlier in my papers, I mentioned many times etheric clouds from the universe. I guess I wasn't too far off.

When I was a young man in the gambling business, I was dealing cards in American Falls, Idaho. There was an old man there that used to put tar paper under his shirts or coats to protect himself from the cosmic rays. Everybody thought he was crazy, including me. Maybe he was right. Also, a German scientist by the name of Wilhelm Riech, who fled from Germany and Hitler, came to the United States, and ended up in jail, where he died of a broken heart. The reason he went to jail was he made, and was selling, an argon energy box. This box was the size of a telephone booth, and had layers of some material he made up all around it on the outside. The American Medical Association had him arrested, and then sent to jail for not having approval. I guess Sun-block can not come in the shape of a telephone booth.

THE EVOLUTIONIST III

After watching the killer whales chasing and eating seals in the tide waters of Alaska, and actually swimming up in the shallow water of the beach and risking being stranded while trying to get a seal-meal, I wondered about the many different sounds that the seals are able to make. True, most of them only sound like a warning to humankind, but to one another, the noises made by the seals mean a great deal more.

Utterances which are made by almost all living creatures mean much more than humankind are able to comprehend. Talking goes much farther into our past than I believe we can conceive. A glare in the eyes of another is an instant warning to pay attention or run. A blank expression brings pity. A smile makes another happy. A yawn means give me time to think it over. We all know what screaming means, and a cat's purring gets the cat a cuddle.

Now that we can talk, we need to spend more time in acquainting ourselves with the other animals and the rest of creation, learning how they communicate, instead of fighting over who will control the populations, the gold, diamonds, or oil. It's time we enjoyed what we have, and understand the feelings of all.

THE EVOLUTIONIST III

It seems that in order to expose the intelligence of a new way of thinking, sometimes it is only necessary to bend the old way of thinking, or the thought, just a little. It may even be that just one word needs to be changed. Sometimes, an argumentative side is taken by one side of the mind, against some thought it has accepted. It is much easier to re-design the thought than it is to create a new thought along the same idea. Recreation is always much easier than creation.

THE EVOLUTIONIST III

It's impossible not to realize what is taking place! We are born and live, with luck, to be seventy years old. Why They, whoever They are, have only given humankind an average of seventy years to live, is beyond me. A turtle, a parrot, and an elephant live over one hundred years.

THE EVOLUTIONIST III

I'm not a very fast reader. In fact, I may even be a slow reader. I believe the cause of this is that I'm studying at the same time that I'm reading.

THE EVOLUTIONIST III

I have been dancing around the brain for close to a year now. I have read writings from the mid-sixteen hundreds describing brain and its components, and how scientists are trying to explain what they can about what makes all creation operate, or more basically, run.

When I read Joseph le Conte, I felt he had the best way of telling me what brain consisted of, and how it operated. Two things made up the foundation of brain in the beginning. They were medulla and thalamus. Le Conte described medulla as the central matter of an organ, and that part which supplies, or controls, cardiovascular activities and respiration: the basics of life itself. Medulla also is referred to as the basic medulla, or central region of parenchyma cells, or pith in the stem of plants. These two explanations expose medulla as being the basic life of flesh and plants, including trees. It's also referred to as Paul Kammerer's "life sap".

Next, we take into consideration the noun "thalamus". This word also is described to support both flesh and plant, or tree, life. The thalamus is described as the larger portions of the brain stem, which is a major sensory coordinating area. Also, the thalamus is described as the sensory receptacle of a flower.

Medulla and thalamus seem to, in other words, be the basic makeup of brain in both flora and fauna: flesh and plant. Soon, I feel, we shall uncover more of what the two are a part of, although

THE EVOLUTIONIST III

flora and fauna seem to pretty well cover the scope of the living, except for the atmosphere.

Medulla often appears as a lone noun. However Medulla Oblongata is often used in describing medulla in connection with brain stem, or the hind-most part of brain. Brain stem could be considered as the basic medullary matter encased in an oblong sheath. It may also contain the thalamus.

THE EVOLUTIONIST III

I had a logger friend who lived near Roberts, Montana, and was working in Cooke City, Montana, where I had one of my outfitting businesses. One day, he came over and asked me if I wanted to buy a bay gelding horse. I asked him the price, and he told me five hundred. I knew the horse, and that he was well broke, but just like every other horse, there's a secret to him.

Stoney's secret was that he knew how to untie knots, and I don't mean simple ones, I mean any knot. His name, Stoney, didn't stay with him long around my guides. Right away his name was changed to Houdini, the escape artist.

Houdini was a real escape artist. In fact, after he untied his own rope from the hitching rail, he would untie all the rest of the horses.

I finally put him on a chain with snaps on both ends, and this stopped his tricks. I could see that it really bothered him, so once in a while I would put him on a lead rope that had to be tied, and he would perk right up, and untie himself and a few of his friends right away. Everything was fine until I would put him back on the chain. As soon as I did that, his personality would change. He seemed to look forward to going into the mountains and use the bit. Anything but the chain with the snaps.

THE EVOLUTIONIST III

𝕀 imagine Goethe's words, spoken by Faust, would cover most my ways of putting words on paper.
>
> Be not a tinkling fool in your address!
> Common sense and truth don't need
> Either art or much display;
> Why hunt high-sounding words indeed,
> If you have something true to say?
> Those speeches filled with tinsel words which try
> To fool humanity with childish prattle,
> Are lifeless as the misty winds which sigh,
> And through the withered leaves in autumn rattle!

THE EVOLUTIONIST III

When I search for the beginning, I must realize the future. On both sides of me, I have a question. The past and the future?

God never told me there was a left and a right! Now that I know, I have security.

Who really cares about the beginning or the end? If there are any!

THE EVOLUTIONIST III

𝕴 have, at last, come to the realization that I have a poor understanding of grammar. I'll try to hold, or keep it down to about seven lines. Two thousand words in each line.

THE EVOLUTIONIST III

It appears lithic is the study of humankind and its relationship to the construction of items that could be used as tools for any benefit. A rock in hand and a hard surface to strike it against could possibly be one of animal's, defined as mankind's, earliest accomplishments. Probably, the club came next.

Undoubtedly, we learned many things from other forms of animals that live by our side, and often use our bodies for a source of food for their energy. From the many different shapes we have evolved through, and the surroundings we have been exposed to, we have undoubtedly learned to eat and survive on almost everything. It has only been a matter of being able to get to it, no matter what type body it comes in.

I can imagine that our source of food had much to do with the tools we constructed. In our earliest history we had pre-built caves, streams and the atmosphere. Fruit and plants required only to be pulled or picked. Maybe a rock to stand on so Eve could reach the apple was our first tool. The saying, "Neccessity is the mother of invention", is so true. Tools were first used as a means of getting food, and then a means of getting at the food. Later, the rock and club became weapons used to keep others away from our food.

This same thing is going on today with our brothers in creation. The chimpanzee uses a twig to get termites out of a small hole the termite may live in. You can bet your life that we did the same thing. A sea gull picks up a clam in the surf and then flies into

THE EVOLUTIONIST III

the air and drops it on rocks, and then glides down to eat it. We only wade in the surf, pick up the clam, wade back to shore, and slam it against a rock. We've learned to shake a limb for fruit, rather than picking them one at a time.

A short time ago, I read about a place in India, where they are overrun by the monkey population. On one occasion, there were a lot of monkeys who had been stealing the apples in an orchard. With only two hands, and small at that, they could only take two apples, at most, at a time. But it seems there was one monkey who was smarter than the rest; he picked up a plastic bag and carried it into the orchard, then ran off with a bag full of apples.

THE EVOLUTIONIST III

𝕬ndt von Hipple, in his book, Human Evolutionary Biology, states on pages 85 and 86, "Apparently, a random insertion of viral DNA just happened to hit an important germ cell (sperm or egg) from which all humans, chimps, and gorillas descend (even a worldwide epidemic caused by the same virus could never have entered and persisted within the ancestral germ cell of all three species by chance - let alone at the exact same chromosonal site). Many other molecular comparisons as well as our undeniable similarity in anatomy and physiology, suggests that humans, chimps, and gorillas really do belong within the same genus. But there is understandable reluctance to recognize such close kinship between humans and mere wild beasts - 'in his image', sounds so much more dignified."

This same random DNA has inserted itself throughout the history of life. Your favorite pet seems to act almost human. To another species of the human race, his pet bird seems to have the same characteristic, "If my bird could only talk." Another of our humankind would pray for their plant to tell the story of life. We are all connected. Satisfy yourself with existing as a member of creation, with an unending reappearance as life goes on.

Transfiguration fuels the universe.

THE EVOLUTIONIST III

At this moment, I feel that creation is enveloped in an atmospheric stage of mentality for understanding the meaning of being. By this, I mean we seem to have passed partially through the stage of physical evolution, and are, at the present time, still on the adventuristic and futuristic trail of learning what we are supposed to be doing. As soon as we stop physically fighting, we can continue our process of physical evolution, and develop a body designed for friendship, not a muscular frame designed to carry a club.

THE EVOLUTIONIST III

𝕀 feel that we have spent more time in the ocean's waters than we have on land. "We bounced along well below sea level long before the planet earth's surface cooled. Our limbs, in the beginning of our aquatic life, were thread-like; yet we could maintain a direction." These were the words of Ernst Haeckel, in the 1800's.

THE EVOLUTIONIST III

Gain and loss mean nothing to evolution; they only mean change, which evolution always has in mind.

THE EVOLUTIONIST III

When I was a youngster, we used to have what was known as a crystal set. These crystal sets consisted of a small crystal rock, maybe a half-inch in diameter, a steel rod about three inches long and an eighth of an inch in diameter, a needle-like wire wrapped around the tip of the rod, with the tip of the wire sticking out at an angle about one-half inch. The rod was mounted so that it could swivel, so you could touch the tip of the wire any place on the side or top of the crystal rock. There was also a set of ear phones. There were no batteries or electrical hook-ups, and yet, when the needle touched the right spot on the crystal rock, you could hear the local radio stations through the ear phones.

The reason for the crystal set coming too mind was my continual search for brain in its microscopic being. Perhaps brain could exist of nothing, and receive just as the crystal set does.

For some reason, the medulla continually exposes itself in the writings of scientists. Many days will pass as I search deeper into the natural study of being, and medulla will not be mentioned; and then, all at once, there it is again. As I thought about the crystal rock in the crystal set, for some reason I thought about the medulla. I have never been able to locate any information concerning the essence of medulla. The closest I have been able to come is marrow. It is said that true love can melt the marrow. Marrow seems to be, or take the place of, medulla, and a vital or essential part; the essence; the "goodness".

THE EVOLUTIONIST III

Medulla, as I've stated before, is what seems to be settled for by early scientists, as the beginning of brain. Medulla and marrow, in many cases, are referred to as being the same thing. The Oxford English Dictionary states, basically; marrow is a companion, fellow worker, partner, mate; then goes on; a husband or wife, and concludes saying; a thing which makes a pair with another. Perhaps this last statement is the answer.

Marrow is also referred to by many names which mean the same as medulla. Medulla merz is one. Medulla merah is another. Medulla, on the other hand, is referred to as the marrow of bones; also, spinal marrow. Also, the substance of the brain. The inward medulla, or marrow of brain. As you can see, and I could go on with this, there seems to be a real connection between medulla and marrow, or these two words, concerning brain. The word brain might be described as "marrow, the pith or heart of the growth at the top of a date-palm". Or as Paul Kammerer put it, "brain sap".

THE EVOLUTIONIST III

In all animals, a certain amount of friendship exists which could be explained as lonesomeness. Being lonesome can bring about friendship quicker than most situations. Two outstanding examples of this are Robinson Crusoe, and the bird man of Alcatraz. Naturally, when two beings come together as friends they become companions. Companions desire to expose their feelings to each other, and continually try to expose these feelings to one another by some sort of language. Human sign language is a perfect example.

My point in this paper is the development of the sentences used in spoken languages. Two people speaking different languages have to use more words to explain something, than a mere, simple one word order. A simple one word order is well understood when both speak the same language. These confused languages could have been one of the reasons for such long sentences. Salutations by gestures were undoubtedly our first means of greeting one another. The one word could have been used, like, "Hello". And then, "Hello, there". And after this, "Hello there. How are you?"

A sentence has been created because we can talk, not because we should say it that way. "Hello", in actuality, is all that is needed.

Some humans like to talk, and say more than is necessary, in order to give the impression that they know more.

THE EVOLUTIONIST III

Humankind, in truth, seems to be too good for the world they have to work with. They seem to be in complete control of everything, except the elements. Some of these, such as raging rivers, fire, and others which humankind seem to have slight control over now. And this control seems to get better by the day.

I wonder how long it will be before we are going to be able to handle the job of being an all-out God?

THE EVOLUTIONIST III

When we consider Heaven, or the hereafter, we must consider the results of what we should expect when the time of arrival presents itself.

I should prefer, myself, the future of rebirth, if possible, and continue my search for the reason I could have rebirth.

THE EVOLUTIONIST III

Mind - consciousness as an element, contrasted with matter: Brain.

THE EVOLUTIONIST III

As we pollute the earth with our waste, we are creating our own grave. The meaning of waste goes far beyond what is excreted from our body today. Waste includes our most deadly enemy, atomic waste. Waste goes on through its meaning to anything which is not wanted, by any individual, any longer. This waste is then thrown aside or taken to an area where it is, in mass, either buried or hauled to another area, where some is recycled, and the rest is once again stashed in a cache, out of sight, by those who have taken on the duty of protecting this waste, so that it may not return to harm its creator: sort of like Frankenstein's Monster.

However, there doesn't seem to be any real way of doing this. No matter where the waste is placed, it seems to still create millions of germs, which are not healthy, and soon return and cause ill health and growth, not as an evolutionary result, but with the addition to our bodies of physical and mental disorders which are hindering our natural process of life.

The result of trying to hide, or cache, the waste is not the answer. The only true, safe answer is to eliminate waste whenever and wherever possible. In my estimation, it is not difficult to discover what might be determined as the best way to get rid of part of it, would be not to create it in the first place. There are many things we could do without.

Junk mail could be one of our most important problems. It used to be that the junk mail could be used to start fires. However,

THE EVOLUTIONIST III

today's rules forbid open burning, or require special permits or hours to burn. And usually, this permit is not for paper or cardboard. We pay for our mail service and yet we cannot forbid delivery of this junk mail. It's against the law for the post office not to deliver it, yet most do not want it. Proof of this is in the trash receptacles at the post offices. The rest of the proof is at the dump or recycling plants.

Our main concern should be that trees make paper, and the forests are going away fast. Not only do trees make paper, but they also make oxygen out of the carbon dioxide we exhale after digesting the oxygen in our lungs.

What might even be better would be to annihilate humankind, and then we wouldn't need junk mail. That would make things tougher on the trees, though, as they wouldn't have our carbon dioxide to breathe.

THE EVOLUTIONIST III

While studying Ernst Haeckel's, The Riddle of the Universe, and Psychic Gradations, in chapter seven, page 115, I suddenly had the feeling that when I transpire, it's going to be more fun to attempt reconciliation with the "living", than it has been attempting to understand my future. In other words, for those who live as cells, both singular and multiple, I am sure that their effect on creation's existence is much more than creation's effect on these cells.

On page 114, Haeckel states, "The most important step in the gradual construction of the reflex mechanism is the division into three cells; in the place of the simple connecting bridge we spoke of, there appears a third independent cell; the soul-cell, or ganglionic cell; with it appears also a new psychic function, unconscious presentation, which has its seat in this cell. The Stimulus is first concluded from the senitive cell to this intermediate presentative or psychic cell, and then issued from this to the motor muscular cell as a mandate for movement. These tri-cellular reflex organs are preponderately developed in the great majority of the invertebrate."

Could this be Le Conte's medulla, the thalamus and the gangloid that make up brain, which is at work in its simplest stage?

THE EVOLUTIONIST III

I understand, after reading <u>The Webster Third International Dictionary</u>, that a "cake eater" is an effeminate, party-going dandy, or what is commonly know as a "tea hound". I can believe that many of the males and females of our species could lean towards being a "cake eater". The scale of physical and mental sex life sometimes becomes very balanced in how a person accepts life. Some, or most, are born with the feeling and educated that it is "wrong". Sometimes education is not really education, but simply the way the educator believes.

THE EVOLUTIONIST III

It's the desire of, or for, being that forces life. Life is digested, like a log in the cabin fire. In fact the fire is Life. What remains is ash, and the ash is digested by the physical forms, from one cell to man. Energy is the result of ambition.

THE EVOLUTIONIST III

If you don't feel life has improved for all, how many can remember catalogs and slick magazines in the outhouses?

THE EVOLUTIONIST III

I was watching the dolphins on the television last night, and suddenly a sort of enlightenment came into mind concerning the friendship between the dolphins and humankind.

For several thousands of years, humankind have had dogs as companions and friends. They have been so close to us that we now take them as a part of the family. In fact, if your dog passes on it is like losing a part of the family. Some folks even have funerals for their dogs at pet cemeteries. Some dogs wear little, special-made clothes to keep them warm, and even styled to catch the eye of friends and other dogs.

This sort of thing hasn't taken place with the dolphins, but perhaps, in the future, someone who lives by the sea will have a pet dolphin, to which they can give some special care. Perhaps it will be seen wearing some special wet suit for cold weather and water.

When I see how the dolphins are attracted to humankind, and how friendly they are, and how they seem to enjoy playing with those who tend them, I have the feeling there is some mental attraction in place. It has only been since the development of underwater diving gear, unlike the old-style, cumbersome diving gear with the hoses, lead shoes, and brass helmets, that the dolphins have shown such attraction to humans. Since mankind have gone underwater in such a large way, these mammals have steadily become more friendly.

It suddenly came to me that humankind, in their past,

actually lived in this same water-world with the dolphin. I wonder if perhaps, even though our bodies were shaped differently when we lived underwater than they are now, and we breathed through gills instead of lungs, if the dolphins somehow seem to recognize something about us that brings back memories from the past of how our friendship might have been, when we too, lived in the wonderful world of water.

THE EVOLUTIONIST III

𝔇isregarding the Mosaic legend, and its six-day creation of our planet earth and all of its' inhabitants, I will attempt, for those who may and I hope do accept it, a scientific exposure and foundation of our planet, and its relationship to the sun.

Copernicus was born February 19, 1473, at Torun, Poland. Nicolaus Copernicus, after attending universities at Cracow, Poland, and at Bologna, and Padua, Italy, returned to Frauenburg, Poland, where he was elected a canon of the Catholic Cathedral, a post ensuring lifelong security.

After becoming increasingly dissatisfied with earth-centered ideas of the universe, he spent many years developing the theory that the earth, and the other planets of our solar system, revolved around the sun, instead of their revolving around the earth. Not until 1540 did he consent to the publication of his complete work, <u>On the Revolutions of the Celestial Spheres</u>. Three years later, Nicolaus Copernicus passed on, May 24, 1543.

THE EVOLUTIONIST III

𝕰 volution is the best bet you have going, even if there is a life in heaven, where we live together, forever. I can not understand how I could live forever. There are too many unanswered, truthwise questions. Through evolution, you are automatically attached physically to everything. Mentally, we are smarter than an eye for an eye. We realize that we exist together, and that it is merely individual tribes who consider their's to be the ideal life, and try to gain control.

One votable, for the people, government. Use this to show power. You have already seen it work, and proof is not needed.

Vote!

THE EVOLUTIONIST III

We are all destined to pay for our time. We acquire these payments for Being. One daily payment we are destined to make for life is the one we have to make at least twice a day to our stomachs. The other is made the easy way, when we sleep, our brain is paid with oxygen to "eat".

THE EVOLUTIONIST III

𝔄 dunghill of vanity is the most ideal place for chapmen (salesmen) to huckster over.

THE EVOLUTIONIST III

Most of the species that make up creation seem to be self centered. Undoubtedly, this self-centeredness is caused, in most cases, and is, in fact, a means of survival. Even though you seldom see a squirrel play with a rabbit, you will see a dog play with a cat. Perhaps this is the result of being raised in civilized surroundings.

It seems that ducks and geese should live together. The next time you see a flock of either, you will see that they eat and live in separate groups. Ravens live with ravens, owls live with owls, quail live with quail, and even trout only live with their own kind. If rainbows live in one stream, cutthroats will live somewhere else, that is, if they aren't planted in the same stream. You'll never see different species of rabbits together. Cottontails don't play with, or mate with, jackrabbits. Certain snakes kill other snakes.

To the contrary, any cow will live with any other breed of cow. In fact, cows will live with almost anything that won't kill them. It seems as though mankind have got the wool pulled over the cows' eyes, though.

It looks as though basic colors can make a difference with the human race. But this is slowly going away.

I can believe that if the different nationalities and colors studied each other, instead of themselves, we'd all get along much better. After all, we've all got the same problems.

THE EVOLUTIONIST III

Mistakes are often thought of as something one should disregard. This is very much untrue. Mistakes have been developed into some of our greatest achievements.

In Bill Calvin's book, <u>How Brains Think</u>, he was telling about a raven picking up a clam and flying into the air and dropping the clam on a rocky area three times before it broke open. The raven was then able to eat the innards. Bill Calvin asked, was this act instinctive behavior, or learned by trial and accidental success, or intelligently innovative? Did some ancestral raven contemplate the problem and then guess the solution?

I have seen both ravens and sea gulls do this same thing. Grab a clam, fly into the air, drop it, and then fly down and eat it. I believe the birds had to first know the shell contained food. This was undoubtedly discovered by birds finding clams washed up on the beach, the shell drying out, half opened, exposing the clam inside. Also, I am sure that the birds watched other animals eat the clams before they tried them, especially the otter. The earliest possible solution to the fly-and-drop method could have been discovered by a bird flying with the clam to be by itself, where it could peck and pry to get the meal. By accident, the clam was dropped, and when the bird flew down to retrieve it, the shell had broken, and the meal was exposed. It wouldn't take a rocket scientist to see that this was an easier way to have dinner. Accidents have presented many of our prized solutions.

THE EVOLUTIONIST III

As I have written before, I have seen many different designs in the way trees have been forced to grow. When I say forced, this seems to be brought about by any particular tree having to surrender to the location where the seed landed, and it will be forced to live here for its lifetime. The only possible change in location might be forced by a flood, and the tree survives in a new place, down the river, or some human takes a liking to the tree and transplants it.

The "Candle Stick Cypress" will grow very tall and straight as an arrow, always. However, all other trees seem to have a dislike for wind. They seem to grow bent from the wind, and some will grow very few limbs on the side from which the wind comes. I've seen them with no limbs on this side.

THE EVOLUTIONIST III

We've never really broken off. Still, we devour what is presented. In most places we breathe air, the same air we've breathed for thousands of millions of years. We could, and probably will, develop into a bi-lunged vertebrate. By this, I mean lungs and gills. With these two, we may be able to develop (evolve) a means of breathing the atmosphere of space.

THE EVOLUTIONIST III

If it weren't for problems, we'd never get smart.

THE EVOLUTIONIST III

𝕴 told myself this morning that I would only write about what pertained to life. Right now, I'm going to write what should explain the benefits of both religion and science. Both, in reality, are scientific. One is just trying to out perform the other. Both pertain to the same thing, and both have flaws. Those who are in the game, on both sides, are primarily interested in the facts that both sides contain. While there are others who only want to pocket the purse.

In their infancy, both drew conclusions that were later discarded. Religions changed them to mythology and science reprimanded their authors. Both science and religion are striving to create an explanation for life. Basically, both are in the same boat.

As time proceeds, we will see that both religion and science will become one. There have been many great scientists who have, and have had, a God. There have also been many great religious followers who have become great scientists. Yes, both have suffered the consequences of their associates for being in sort of a middle-of-the-road situation.

Pope John Paul II is suffering through this same situation now, for his belief in the fact of evolution. However, in future years, just as many others before him, he will be immortalized for his gift concerning the honest way he feels about evolution.

I'm sure Darwin, too, had his God, just as many other evolutionists do. God is only a word to be used as verbally explaining to others what we feel to be our protector and connection

THE EVOLUTIONIST III

with what we do not understand.

The purse snatchers have used this word, God, as a means of controlling the masses, who, as many, only want to understand. However, due to the fact that I used to travel with the thieves, I can fully understand that they, too, have their "God".

In some instances, the law is against having a God, In other instances, a tribe or country is founded on "their" God.

It has always been an easy answer for going to war!

THE EVOLUTIONIST III

There is no doubt in my mind that there still exists many direct descendants of the dinosaurs and great reptiles which roamed the planet earth in its early stages. Some of these descendants should be the rhinoceroses, hippopotami, elephants, and some, or perhaps all, of the whale families. There are undoubtedly many more which were, and are, descended from the small dinosaurs, and perhaps even the ostrich. When it comes to the real answer, which truly solves the riddle , "Where do we come from?", it is very simple; "each other".

I just can't believe the dinosaur population, or species, were entirely eliminated from the planet by an asteroid or comet hitting earth. And while we're on this subject, Ernst Haeckel feels that the earth was slowly created from the sun and came into existence as it was built up from the gaseous material which is radiated from the sun. When earth grew large enough, the centrifugal force and weight let the planet slowly drift out into its own orbit, where it is today. As far as any planet exploding in a so-called "Big Bang", I also feel that bangs, not so big, have been going on for a long, long time, and are the results of comets and asteroids striking different planets which populate the universe.

These large stone-like objects and meteors, or meteoroids, could also strike any planet. The hunks, or stone-like objects that the television shows us sailing through the universe, had to be the results of such collisions. Their shapes are the result of broken

THE EVOLUTIONIST III

objects. If they were comets or asteroids, their bodies would be round, not like broken pieces of stone, as the television often shows them heading for earth.

THE EVOLUTIONIST III

Osmosis is the ability of a substance to pass through a semipermeable membrane. Osmics deals partially with the science, and sense, of smell.

In other words, when you naturally breathe through your nose, vapors carrying various odors in the atmosphere upon intake by your lungs are drawn through your nose. The vapor permeates cells in the nose and pass through membrane with nerves, which relay the smell to brain. Brain, like a computer, diagnoses the smell and tells the body.

These odors are actually digested by the lungs. This same action takes place merely by breathing and digesting oxygen in the lungs.

THE EVOLUTIONIST III

It seems to me that those who are shooting rockets into space had better be careful. After all the large projectiles are passing right through "heaven".

THE EVOLUTIONIST III

Open your heart to nature, and your mind will see the future.

THE EVOLUTIONIST III

When I first stumbled across the name orange-man, or orangemen, I was in search of the name and information concerning the biped, animal, orangutan. When I use the dictionary many times I will check words that are spelled like the word that I have been searching for, or nearly the same.

When I found the name orangutan, there were only a few words in the dictionary above it; one of them was orange-man, and the other was orange-men. This word or name was described as follows: after the prince of Orange, the late William III (William I 1533-1584 was also Prince of Orange). William I Duke of Normandy, William I King of Prussia and emperor of Germany, William II King of England, William III King of England, Scotland, and Ireland, William the Conqueror was also William I the Duke of Norway. I'll say one thing for the orange people, they must have been the toughest tribe of all in the times of the Vikings, and feared by all.

If you will check a globe or map you will see most of the ancestors of William the I, II, III and IV came from areas of the Orange haired and light complected Vikings. These species of the human race had very orange hair, and light orange-white, sometimes freckled, skin, and must have been an original human species of that area.

It's very hard to find information on these tribes of people, however if you will look around in your daily travels you will find that there are a great many more of them than you realized. Not that they are different than any other species of the human race but I feel sure they are from the tribes which were originally situated in the far north on the European Continent. Also I feel that the Vikings were their true forefathers.

There are no real red heads, reddish-orange maybe, but not true red. Blondes, too, are a more faded orange. White is almost always connected with Albino. Many people call Swedish people blond haired, also there are supposed to be blond people all over the territory of the Orange-haired people. I am sure I will be finding more information about the silent orange-men as my search continues.

Incidentally the word Orange-man is also described as being members of a secret protestant society, organized in northern Ireland in 1795. Could it have been possible they were orange-men which were a tribe from ancient Normandy?

William I, 1027-1087, the Duke of Normandy invaded England and killed Harold the Harefoot, the King of England at the battle of Hastings in the 1066. William I became the King of England at that time and I am sure that the name, William the Conqueror fit him well. William the Conqueror and his entire army of Orangemen were undoubtedly those who brought orange hair genes to the British Isle. It could be that the fighting, orange-haired Irish-men came down from the north, too. They were smaller, but just as tough.

THE EVOLUTIONIST III

Could it be the orange-men have been generated beside the orange-haired orang'-utan, just as the white-man, and the black-man have been generated beside the black-haired apes. Maybe there were orange hair cells, and black hair cells. Seems like there are sure a lot of them around today. No wonder they call it a family tree!

The word orange, besides meaning an edible fruit, also means the name of a ruling family in the ancient history of the Netherlands, The House of Orange.

It's a funny thing there are no listings for black-man or white-man in . . . I just stopped to check and found blackman in Websters Third New International Dictionary,

blackman n. l: black. 2: an evil spirit: boogeyman, devil.

Boy, that's a little tough to handle. Maybe they mean boogeyman that boogies. Let's get on with it. Black man is also in the Oxford English Dictionary.

black man 1. A black man having a black or very dark skin. Also black men are "Pearls in beauteous Ladies eyes".

White man has no listing in Webster International Dictionary. I guess they said enough about the black-men. White man is in the Oxford English Dictionary.

white-man 1 A man clothed in white, a surplice chorister (a white man dressed in white, singing in a choir).

I think I'd rather be a boogie man. In fact, the ancient medicine men were also boogie men. So much for the dictionaries, at least they have black, orange, and white listed as men, and not

THE EVOLUTIONIST III

Neanderthals. I just checked to see if they had yellow-man. They only had yellow-haired.

yellow-haired. Having yellow (flaxen, auburn, or golden) hair. "Let the yellow-haired Giaours view his horsetail with dread."

This sounds like a man from China losing his "pigtail".

Looks like the dictionaries are starting to loosen up a little. They've even got a four letter word starting with "F" in most of them now, that means 'generate'. It's nice to have a little entertainment now and then.

THE EVOLUTIONIST III

Why is it that in dictionaries it takes so many words to mean one thing, and then only one word to mean so many things? It seems to me that certain people who claim to be educated in certain ways, work for publishers of our dictionaries and seem to elaborate more than needed on certain subjects or words. Soon others tire of their wasting time and the original meaning for the subject, or word is lost and another word has taken its place, leaving the student or person in search befuddled.

    Cortex- the outer layer of gray matter over most of the dicotyledonous plants located between the stele and epiderms .
    Cortex- the outer layer of gray matter over most of the brain.
    Cortex- loosely any layer of stem tissue external to xylem.
    Cortex- pharmacy- the bark or rind of a plant.
    Pith- the soft spongy tissue in the center of certain plant stems.
    Pith- the soft core of various other things, as of a bone or feather.
    Pith- the spongy, fibrous tissue lining the rind and surroundings the section of an orange or grapefruit.
    Pith- the essential part; substance gist.
    Pith- of great pith and moment.
    Pith- strength, vigor, force.
    Pith- to remove the pith from a plant stem.

THE EVOLUTIONIST III

Pith- to pierce or sever the spinal cord.

See what I mean!

THE EVOLUTIONIST III

Solomon, nearly two thousand years before Darwin, stated, "My heart tells me, concerning the fate of man, that God will expose them to the fact that humankind are related to all creation.

For that which happens to man, happens to all creation. As one passes on, the other passes on; All receive the same reward.

No person can tell another the spirit of man goes up, and the spirit of the rest of creation goes down.

For this reason, I feel that man should be happy in his own work, for who shall bring mankind to see what shall be after them."

THE EVOLUTIONIST III

Could it be that the reason the other species of animals do not have strokes is the simple matter of not having the complexities of the human brain? I have always felt that the simpler something is, the stronger it is. Look at our Constitution.

THE EVOLUTIONIST III

We have to walk many miles, in order to advance one single step forward.

THE EVOLUTIONIST III

One thing we do know for sure, everyone and everything must have enjoyed eating brain/marrow. Thousands of crushed skulls, with only the brain pan remaining, have been found, mostly in caves, indicating they were more than a source of energy. The same is true for those who love the marrow of the bones. Both must have been a real delicacy.

To get past the blocked trail of brain, medulla and marrow, a person must disregard the containers in which medulla and marrow seem to exist in. I forgot to mention that both exist in vegetation, as pith, and both exist as brain. And by eliminating the containers they live in, we are left with medulla and marrow. These two, along with pith, are quite a question. I would like to know, what they are made of?

Marrow has many words which describes it, because it is able to be seen and eaten by all of mankind, with all of their languages and dialects to refer to it as . . . At least all, or most, of the words meaning marrow begin with the letter "m". Medulla, on the other hand, sometimes is mentioned as being transparent. The Oxford Dictionary tells us that the real structure of the the primitive nerve fiber appears to be a tube composed of homogeneous membrane, containing a delicate, soft, pulpy, semi-fluid, and transparent material, we can refer to as medulla.

For the first time today, while searching once again for the ever-elusive medulla in the Britannica, I discovered Marshall Hall,

THE EVOLUTIONIST III

(1794-1883). In his 89 years on Earth, Marshall Hall conducted physiological research that gained him renown on the European Continent, and England. He denounced the practice of blood letting in 1830. His discovery, that a headless newt moves when its skin is pricked, led to a series of experiments that he summerized in the paper, "On the functions of the medulla Oblongata - medulla spinalis (Marshall Hall, Brit. IV page 858), and on the Excitomotory system of nerves (1837)". This research gave Hall a basis for his theory concerning reflex action. The headless newt, without a head, contains brain!

If this is true, then what I have said and felt, is also true; that all creation, seen and unseen, must contain brain to exist.

It is kind of how I felt when I began this paper; we must be made up sort of like crystal sets.

Here are a few listings from the Dictionary concerning medulla:

> Medusarian - of, or belonging to, the family medusaria, consisting of the meduase or jellyfish, or an animal of this family. A jellyfish is considered to be an animal.
>
> Medusa - a jellyfish or sea nettle; any one of the soft, gelatinous discophorous hydrozoans.
>
> 1832, Humboldt's travels - The whole sea was covered with a prodigious quantity of medusae. (a few years ago this same thing took place in the ocean in front of my home in

Oregon).

1835, Kirby - They are gelatinous like the medusas and beroes.

1888, Rolleston and Jackson - The ovum is marked as it always is, in Craspedote Meduase.

1882, Callels Natural History - One of the prettiest, free-swimming medosoids is more or less bell-shaped.

1890, Futhergill - free swimming medusoids or craspedota with velum.

Hydrosoa - the various organisms called acalephs, medusae, or jellyfish. Also in singular - hydrozoon.

It seems evident that, in some way, there is a connection, however, I am sure that it could not be Medusa. Medusa was one of three mythical Greek female personages, with snakes for hair, whose look turned the beholder into stone. The one of most note, and the only one mortal, Medusa, was slain by Perseus, and her head fixed on Athena's shield.

In the year, 1668, Phil. Trans. III. 889 He (who knows who) affirms, that the whole Substance called Medulla of Brain and the After-brain is a Heap of Fibers or Vessels.

This is a bad way to end this paper, but it's not the end.

THE EVOLUTIONIST III

I can believe that the planet earth was formed from the etheric mist which surrounds our sun. I can also believe that it grew larger and heavier as it slowly moved away from the sun, to an orbit which was stabilized by the weight and speed of our planet earth.

In this orbit, the planet earth began its cooling process, to present to creation, through which we have evolved, a place to exist and generate. As this process allowed microscopic organisms to become, it has been slowly burning the nucleus away, cooling, and also becoming lighter. As our home becomes lighter, the sun's gravity will slowly pull the planet back into the clutches of the sun, where, in time, the sun will digest what is left; perhaps to let the planet continue on through the same process again.

During this vast life after life of our planet, sun, itself, has been, and still is, traveling in its own galactic orbit through the Milky Way. Perhaps in a trillion or so years, the sun will have proceeded through this same process of cooling and Sun will be our new home. I wonder what we, humankind, and the rest of creation will look like then?

THE EVOLUTIONIST III

Could it have been that sex and its urge could be one of the major causes of physical and mental evolution. Almost everything is over powered by the urge to satisfy sexual desires.

Also could it be that hunger and the need for food for energy and the digestion of all sorts of other Beings, including some so small we don't realize we're eating them when we breathe, could have brought about physical change.

I read once that type A and type B blood are brought about in humans because of some eating flesh, and some eating vegetation. This sounds okay, but a doctor friend of mine told me it was not true. Sounds pretty good though.

THE EVOLUTIONIST III

𝔅y researching in the Old and New Testaments, both will put you in the hands of a god to fear.

Research through the science of evolution will put you in the hands of mesons and cosmic rays.

THE EVOLUTIONIST III

Does learning require memory? Or rather, come through habit?

THE EVOLUTIONIST III

In his book,"The Riddle of The Universe", Ernst Haeckel states;

> "The life of the animal and the plant bears the same universal character of incompleteness as the life of man. This is directly attributable to the circumstance that nature - organic as well as inorganic - is in a perennial state of evolution, change, and transformation. This evolution seems on the whole - at least as far as we can survey the development of organic life on our planet - to be a progressive improvement, an historical advance from the simple to the complex, the lower to the higher, the imperfect to the perfect. I have proved in my <u>General Morphology</u>, that this historical progress - or gradual perfecting (teleosis) - is the inevitable result of selection, and not the outcome of a preconceived design. That is clear from the fact that no organism is perfect; even if it does perfectly adapt itself to its environment at a given moment, this condition would not last very long; the conditions of existence of

THE EVOLUTIONIST III

the environment are themselves subject to perpetual change and they thus necessitate a continuous adaption on the part of the organism".

Haeckel goes on to call Whoever, or Whatever It is that controls the destiny of creation, "The blind controller", instead of the "Provident God".

Mindz (mind's eye) - the inherent mental ability to imagine or remember scenes. Or in opposition, the working of Brain to remember, and then imagine.

In this recourse, Haeckel makes an attempt to do away with any "thing" which might be in control of the destiny of creation. In other words, he is telling us, which is partially a way I personally feel at times, that creation, including humanity, is what is controlling its own destiny. Most of the time, I can go along with this belief, and then I realize that in humankind there is a great amount of self centeredness. In this I mean, and feel, that man does not feel to be his brother's keeper. In fact, if an idea or impulse produces a superior way, a human might conceal it as a personal advantage. Truth of this is when the multitudes line up on one side to develope a power to control the followers, and urge them to overthrow opposition, rather than peacefully demonstrate how creation has been guided to produce for one another.

When Haeckel stated, "the development of organic life on

THE EVOLUTIONIST III

our planet . . . to be a progressive improvement, an historical advance from simple to complex, the lower to the higher, the imperfect to the perfect", he speaks of the improvement of properties that have been ours, not only in the past, but are ours at the present time. If it were not for telepathy, a part of creation who now contain the ability to see, would have not had the desire to see. However, just because we had, or have, no eyes, we were not, or are not, inferior. Nothing has been simple, lower or imperfect. Every part which has been used to better our being has been advantageous to all of creation. No matter Supreme Creator, God, or whatever. On this same subject, how is it possible for those who want to improve our relationship, to argue and take sides over a question which is supposed to advance our civilization, and life in its entirety. Scientists have shown us fossil remains which we understand and believe to be our ancestral remains, and yet we argue over which is which, and the method in which they transformed, or transpired. The extinction of the dinosaurs, at the present time, seems to be of utmost concern, and yet, why should we make monkeys out of ourselves, in the eyes of all, and especially the creationists, who endeavor to suffocate those who expound the process of evolution in their own thoughts.

    Whether there is or is not, in the case of many things, makes little difference. We are here, we understand, by the help of those who have spent their lives searching the riddle of life, yet we are unable to get a complete expose of life's meaning or purpose. One thing we have to do, for sure, is to realize the moral situation of existence. Without one another, what could be the use?

It also appears that during the time Haeckel wrote The Riddle of The Universe, some of the scientists seem, for some reason, to have felt that there were three great epochs in the organic history of our planet. These were the primary, which controled thirty million years, the secondary, which controlled the next eleven million years, and the third, the tertiary, which has controlled the recent three million years.

When a person makes a mistake in one instance, due to what others have said, we must still very much appreciate the time they have spent on the subject. At the time of Haeckel's statement of these three periods, interest on the subject was in its infancy. Today we know, just as Haeckel knew then, by the words of the so-called modern scientists and DNA, that these periods were like billions instead of millions. I, personally, have a tribolite, which is supposed to be five hundred million years old.

Our future holds many similar discoveries, just as our past has. What we see and hear today will undoubtedly be as Haeckel's; simple, lower, and imperfect. Just as trying to divide the history of creation into the first, the second, and the tertiary epochs.

One epoch is much more comfortable to deal with, just as simple, lower and imperfect things are much easier to deal with. When we are dealing with the question, "Is there or isn't there a God?", and with the problem of having no foundation for either

THE EVOLUTIONIST III

answer; rather than lie, which is neccessary to do in either answer, it is much better to shrug your shoulders, and peer into the heavens.

THE EVOLUTIONIST III

𝕱or several years I have felt that the penis and the testes had more to do with our bodies than creating sperm for generation. Somehow, I always had a feeling that these organs had to be connected or coupled in some way to brain. After spending years thinking about this, and many hours of tracking leads from word to word, I suddenly found the answer on Friday, the 13th of November, 1998.

The epithelium is a cellular tissue that lines a cavity, consisting of one or more layers of cells forming a sheet. The sheet, practically unbroken by an intercellular substance of either smoothly extended, or much folded on a basement membrane. This is compacted and serves to enclose and protect pans of the bodies of both male and female sexes, and form the most essential part of the sense organs, which produce secretions or excretions to function in assimilation and birth.

I guess that I will now have to find the connection or nerve line between the epithelium and the thalamus, that part of brain that operates the sensory system.

THE EVOLUTIONIST III

If God made the earth, and it passed through the stages of being a molten, gaseous sphere, and then cooled to present a place that could support life as we know it, and then made all of the animals, fish, etc., doesn't it seem that he would have made more than just one man?

THE EVOLUTIONIST III

Brain is the only part of your body that does not just hang out and wait for you to decide to eat. The stomach gets sore, and your nerves start twitching, if no food is supplied. And still, they have to wait. Brain just says, "Let's eat".

THE EVOLUTIONIST III

My memories are slowly grinding to dust, as I wear them away.

THE EVOLUTIONIST III

The idea of mass extinction has long been on the lips of humankind. Some wrote about comets striking the earth long ago. Undoubtedly, there were terrible upheavals of our planet as the giant plates, which the crust of the earth is made of, rose and sank as they adjusted their positions. Also, there have been, and still are, the eruptions of the volcanoes, as they blow the the tops off mountains, trying to relieve the pressure from under the giant slabs of earth. Since I was a child, I have listened to the tales of the lost civilization of Atlantis.

I am inclined to believe all of these stories, due to the fascination each presents. I am sure that comets have struck our earth. I am also sure that some mountains have slipped out of sight as the oceans swallowed them up, and at the same time, others rose out of the sea, to be even taller than those which sank.

There were also, undoubtedly, long periods of darkness, and toxic clouds that covered our earth when these catastrophes took place. There are many theories regarding the manner in which the earth was first formed. However, it is here, and we and the rest of creation must exist on it. Also, we must remember those who exist as the nucleus and live under this crust. It has to be true that mass extinctions have taken place as our planet passed through its stages of development. However, I cannot bring myself to believe in the mass extinction of the dinosaurs, just as I cannot swallow the extinction of the entire civilization of Atlantis. Dinosaurs, just as

THE EVOLUTIONIST III

humankind, existed all over the earth. Life covered what we call Mother Earth. Land, sea, and our atmosphere all contain life. Life, or to be, has passed from the etheric atmosphere to where it now stands. If all were lost in the next instant, It, or our Spirit, would put it together again. Even if we were set back further than what our civilization calls, "the beginning for this existence", I am positive we will return, stronger than ever.

On the instance of the Dinosaurs, I think they were made extinct by some sort of catastrophe. I am sure what ever made them, in the first place, would not simply say, "we didn't need them in the first place, we'll just continue on, and forget they ever existed". This is impossible. The Dinosaurs were evolved as a necessity for us to continue the mode of evolution. They were what we evolved into, and they were what this creation evolved out of. They were a major step in evolution, and they still exist in the creational forms which we see today.

There has never been any part of creation that has been made extinct, and not carried forth in our genes to be a part of us now. The reason I know this to be true, is that the tree of life contains, in its makeup, the genes of all who have been. There are none who could be considered to be individual. All of creation might be called one, if we believe this way. If this were true, then it would be impossible to lose any part of the one. If some thing has been, it would have to be. Being is able to overcome all obstacles.

THE EVOLUTIONIST III

It's impossible that who ever put the Universe together and made millions of stars and planets, and then created some of the most beautiful urchins and fish in the sea, and all sorts of reptiles, and mammals almost beyond belief, and birds that could sail and fly through the sky, would only make one man, and then take a rib out of him and make a woman.

I know God created another group of people before Adam. At least that's what the Old Testament says in Genesis 1:26-27-28. But after telling them to subdue the earth and have dominion over the fish of the sea, and the fowl of the air, and over every living thing that moveth upon the earth, that was it. And then God created a real problem The chosen, with their parents, Adam and Eve. After a few pages of Genesis, God realized the mistake and drowned the lot. Once again, He would try, and if it didn't work with Noah and his small family, He was going to forget it all and annihilate the whole thing. That's what he told Isaiah a few thousand years later. But I guess things turned out okay; we're still here.

THE EVOLUTIONIST III

The cracking of boulders and rocks into sand has to do with the contraction and expansion caused by freezing and heating. Once the crack has started, and water seeps in and freezes, the cracking process goes faster. Extreme heat tends to make the crack work from the inside of the rock out.

THE EVOLUTIONIST III

Brain, after passing through the flames which accompanied the beginning of the planet, sought to enclose itself in bodies, which it did. Soon, these cell-like bodies became as we are, and all creation smiles as we continue with designs of the future.

THE EVOLUTIONIST III

The plates were really rattling when the Rocky Mountains were born. Come to think of it, they're still rattling.

THE EVOLUTIONIST III

I can imagine that to go beyond where we are in the study of animals, we are going to have to search deeper than the stratification of ground-up rocks, sand , and the sediment between these layers, which I will call mud. Mud is known by almost all of humankind, and is especially useful to children in many ways; mud balls to throw, mud pies to play house, mud puddles to play in, just mud everything. You could even look like a cannibal by rubbing mud on your face.

There was a very interesting character who lived in Wisdom, Montana, from about 1930 through the 1950's. His surname was Fetty, which was what everyone called him. He owned Fetty's Bar and Restaurant. All the cattle ranchers of the Big Hole Basin hung out there, along with ranch hands and cattle buyers. In the spring, when the mud puddles were everywhere, especially in the dirt streets of the town, Fetty made it a point to sit in front of his bar, on the loafer's bench, and wait for the kids to pass by on their way to Sunday school. When they drew near, he would start tossing nickels, dimes, and even quarters into the puddles of muddy water. The kids, naturally, would forget where they were going, and that they were wearing their Sunday best, and dive in for the loot. Some of the children would take the long route to church so they wouldn't miss out on the fun. In fact, even those that had received spankings for ruining their clothes the previous week would still fall for the quarters.

THE EVOLUTIONIST III

Maybe in one hundred, or five hundred million years, our descendants will be searching the fossil grounds, and find Fetty's teasing coins.

This is just what the world's civilization, today, is finding in the layers of compressed mud and rock. Of course, the scientists have another name for it, but to me and my teach-yourself education, it will always be mud, maybe silt, and rocks. To scientists there are, in my awkward guess, thousands of kinds of mud, and just as many different rocks.

I've never dug through these fossilized places, but I've spent my entire life simply hiking, fishing, and hunting in some of the best fossil-bearing country known to the scientific world. One of the greatest regions for this is from Montana to Mexico, including the Dakotas, Wyoming, Utah, California, Colorado, etc.

To get to the point of this paper, there were very few of what I call "big rocks" in these fossilized layers of earth, which are exposed by time along with nature. Most of them are sedimentary layers, compressed by one another, and at times having the weight of the water on them, which could have been an ocean, miles deep.

Where I have a home at the present time is just the opposite of these layers of sediment. I live in California, in the foothills of the Sierra Nevada mountains, which, in my estimation, extend from Mexico to Canada. I've traveled extensively through this country for seventy years, and only know the geography, or anything else, from personal observation. Books were never the true answer for me.

THE EVOLUTIONIST III

Getting back to this 2,000-mile long pile of rocks, probably the most fascinating part of the great upheaval is Yosemite National Park. There are rocks there that are bigger than a lot of towns. I'm talking about rocks that are not compressed, with layers and designs in them, but just plain-ass, hard rocks.

It is this type of rock that is bringing me closer to what I have to say. Again, I live in the rocky foothills on the Kern River, which has it's beginnings in King's Canyon National Park, where there are rocks the size of a city block.. It travels through the Sequoia National Park, down the Kern River Canyon to Bakersfield, and then, several thousand years ago, swung around and headed north through the San Joaquin Valley, and on to the San Francisco Bay.

While traveling up the Kern River Canyon, about fifteen miles upstream from Kernville, you can see these giant rock mountains, which are slowly fracturing to finally become sand, that will join other sands and "mud" to become layered in the San Joaquin Valley. Perhaps these layers will be compressed under an ocean of water, like this valley used to be. When the oil and water wells are drilled, penetrating this bottom land in the San Joaquin Valley, it, too, is composed of these same fossilized layers.

When I say fossilized, that's exactly what I mean. When it comes to explaining the terrain, it is all either fossilized, or a home for new life. And most of the time, one handful of earth, dirt, will contain both.

THE EVOLUTIONIST III

As I drive up the canyon, especially during a wet winter, the green lichen is thick on the rock cliffs. Once in a while, when a fracture exposes the inside of the rock, you see that it is lichen-free, and is white, red, or maybe blue in color. But soon, the lichen seem to appear, all by itself. Why? It's because these rocks are full of life. Perhaps it is dormant, but I have a feeling it's more like the Grizzly Bear that used to inhabit this country, when they were in hibernation. If a bear can hibernate for an entire winter, or certain fish or frog can hibernate for hundreds of years, then it seems to me that lichen should be able to hibernate indefinitely. Being exposed by a fracture of the rock to the air, sun, and water seems to set it in motion. This motion, and several millions of years, are enough to evolve it into something that may be able to swim, or move on land.

At their beginning, in the rock, or better yet, all through the rock, they are our brothers, and - - - you might say they are <u>Ma</u>sons brought to be by <u>mesons</u>.

Check the dictionary!

Life, in reality, was melted into these rocks for protection, many millions of years ago.

THE EVOLUTIONIST III

All my life , I've seen the signs, "Trust in Jesus". I have no problem with the sign, it's the people who tell you about Jesus, and what he did, that I question.

THE EVOLUTIONIST III

A new generation, in my estimation, should be every twenty years. Possibly, this is where they arrive at twenty-one as a legal age. This means that in one hundred years, there would be five generations.

In one thousand years, there would be fifty generations.

In one hundred thousand years, there would be five thousand generations.

Following this formula, and if my figures are correct, in one million years, there would be fifty thousand generations, and in one billion years, there would be fifty million generations.

Do you really think, if we last that long, that we will be in our same physical shape along with the rest of creation?

THE EVOLUTIONIST III

Most of the time, when we say brain, we are not visualizing brain. When we say brain, we are visualizing how, or what, brain does, not a physical picture of brain.

THE EVOLUTIONIST III

We brought traces of our gills from the sea with us. I wonder if we'll need them again?

THE EVOLUTIONIST III

When you compare bipeds, quadrupeds, fish, reptiles, birds, etc., it is very easy to see and study their mental abilities at work. Everything that exists seems to contain at least one of the similarities that most expose through their daily actions.

George Romanes, in his book, <u>Mental Evolution in Man</u>, published in 1902, explains:

> "If we have regard to emotions as these occur in the brute, we cannot fail to be struck by the broad fact that the area of psychology which they, these brutes, cover is so nearly co-extensive with that which is covered by the emotional faculties of man, which I here name in the order of their appearance through the psychological scale - fear, surprise, emulation (imitate or surpass), pride, resentment, emotion of the beautiful, grief, hate, cruelty, benevolence, revenge, rage, shame, regret, deceitfulness, and moral sense.
>
> When you watch others in creation as they live their daily lives, each will continue to exhibit one and then another of these psychological expressions. By spending time in the observation of creation, a person can

draw themselves nearer to the understanding that we are all related. One is not special or above the other, and to finally realize that you are, truly related to these "others", is eternity understood. In the eyes of God all are created equal."

I saw the worst case of revenge in Dillon, my German Shepherd, that I have ever seen. When he was a pup, one of my other dogs, Wing, a poodle and cocker cross, used to beat him up all the time, for no apparent reason. Dillon carried a fear of Wing since their first fight. Dillon out grew Wing in the first year, yet still had a fear of him. But one day, Dillon decided to fight back, instead of running. He thoroughly beat Wing in the fight. I had to pull him off Wing, it was so bad. From that instant on, he literally brow beat Wing so badly that it was shameful. Dillon not only harassed Wing all of the time, but it was impossible now for anyone to get near the car. Other dogs never bothered Dillon after his first fight. It was a pure act of revenge, on Dillon's behalf. Dillon took advantage of this revenge. In fact, he became so obsessed with this revenge that it changed his personality.

THE EVOLUTIONIST III

When I was a young man I made a deal with God. The deal was I would spend the first half of my life making enough money and gathering enough assets to support my family for the remainder of my life, The rest of my time would be devoted to what I suspected every one could believe in: evolution. It was a little lopsided though. I hustled until 1956, when I published my first works, "The Voice of Creation". I spent several years writing and hustled money on the side. In other words I was moonlighting. At that time I was 33 years old. However, both hustling, reading, and writing all took place until 1996. It was then that I returned to reading and writing and I was in my early seventies. Today, at nearly seventy-five, I am more capable than ever before, due to my experience in both living and observing life, to tell the story of what I have been led to believe and feel to be truthful.

Sometimes assumptions take place on my part. However, most are proven right as I continue to follow the tracks of those who were ahead of me. The trail I have followed will always be ahead, and I'm sure it is the right direction for others who will take the place of those, and me, who only want to feel they have added to the stew of progress and understanding, a means of Being.

THE EVOLUTIONIST III

𝕴n the time before the earth had a crust, what could be called continents were, in reality, clots of elements which had begun to cool on the surface of this flaming, earthen sphere. Our sea, at this time, was a molten mass, which was being showered, as it is today, by cosmic rays.

As the cooling process continued, the crust became thicker and more rigid. However, the pressure below the crust repeatedly erupted, causing the crust to continually shatter and reunite. A solid form was finally constructed to contain the molten nucleus. Only swelling boils blasted as volcanoes.

Our planet earth was obeying the law of progress.

THE EVOLUTIONIST III

Economy is forced to devour some to satisfy others. Is there a difference? Life seems to exist on those who have, and who have not fallen!

THE EVOLUTIONIST III

When it comes down to it, you've got to settle for what God has to offer.

THE EVOLUTIONIST III

There are animals that used to live above ground and that were equipped with eyes. For some reason, these animals went underground to live. In time they changed to a complete underground living, skin has grown over their eyes, and they can no longer see. Other senses have replaced the eyes, which is similar to radar. I wonder, if they returned to the surface, or above ground, how long it would take for them to regain their eyesight?

This same process might be compared to the use of the calculator and the computer. The calculator has taken the place of having to do addition, subtraction, multiplication and division, with a machine instead of using brain. Could it be in the future that many who use this device will no longer understand the basics of arithmetic?

Arithmetic, in the dictionary, is described as; the science or art of computing by positive, real numbers.

The computer goes far beyond the calculator, and could possibly result in more and larger catastrophes.

Are we mentally ascending or descending?

THE EVOLUTIONIST III

I feel more and more deeply that creation will overcome what we feel to be empty space.

We have been able to crawl to the shores and breathe the vaporous air, and dispose of the gills we had been using to refine water into oxygen, when we lived as fish in the water.

What is there that would stop us from evolving into another being able to exist on what space would present to us?

And where do we go from there?

Life presents us with many obstacles, yet even more pleasures. As a fact, there are Beings who are living in the atmosphere and space. They are called cosmic rays or mesons.

THE EVOLUTIONIST III

𝕮 omplete freedom seems to be in sight, maybe plus or minus, these seem to be the rules we go by, plus or minus. Maybe this is, or seems to be, by the way the lawyers work, the LAW of plus or minus.

THE EVOLUTIONIST III

Œvolutionism; the religious science of our future.

THE EVOLUTIONIST III

When I was in Alaska, I wondered what made all the vegetables up there grow so much bigger then they do in the lower states. I understood that they had long winters with no sunshine, and long summers with all sunshine, and that was it. But if you add up our amount of sunshine, we get close to the same amount as Alaska, except it comes at daily intervals throughout the years, instead of one long day, from May to October.

Just a few days ago, it finally came to me, with the help of Arndt von Hipple. Arndt is the author of <u>Human Evolutionary Biology</u>, and lives in Anchorage. "There's more sunshine" he told me. I guess he thought I was smart enough to know what he meant. It took a few days for me to wake up to the real reason things get bigger. They do get more sunshine because they get steady sun shine during the growing time. That is, our vegetables only get twelve hours of sunshine a day and the vegetables in Alaska get twenty four hours of sunshine a day in their growing period, that's twice as much.

It was really a relief to get that problem solved, even if it took me almost thirty years.

THE EVOLUTIONIST III

So that your descendants might be ready for future discoveries, Protista, from the German Protisten, used by the German scientist, Ernst Haeckel in 1868, is explained by the <u>Oxford English Dictionary</u> as : A third Kingdom of organized beings, proposed by Haeckel to include those of the simplest structure, not definitely distinguished as either animals or plants. In other words, the relationship of animals to plants may be joined by another, yet undecided variant of life.

THE EVOLUTIONIST III

Lamarck, the French naturalist, born Jean Baptiste Pierre Antoine de Monet Lamarck, 1744 - 1829, expounded a theory of organic evolution in which he claimed, acquired characteristics of ancestors can be inherited by descendants.

This was an early attempt at expounding the fact of evolution, and how it operates.

THE EVOLUTIONIST III

𝕭eing is the result of spent energy!

THE EVOLUTIONIST III

When a person gets involved with the quark, or meson, or atomic structure, and cosmic rays, they are nearing the world of nothingness, or what may be called the unseen. The atom is made of the protons, electrons, and neutrons. So many of each are what the elements are comprised of. An element is described as, one of the simple substances of which all material bodies are composed. Also, an element is described as a member of the, or our, planetary system.

If all of the above are true, then it is possible, if we go backwards, to get a clearer picture. All material bodies are made up of elements. Elements are members of the planetary system. The elements are made up of atoms. The atom, or atomic structures are made up of protons, electrons, and neutrons. So many of each of these in an atom fabricate different elements. Originally, there were four elements, then five or six, then seventy. Today, there are more than double the seventy elements.

The atom is also connected in some way to the quark, which, in turn, is a part of the meson, which makes up the cosmic ray.

One hundred years ago, the atom was as dark in our minds as the quark, or meson, or cosmic rays are today. I feel sure that without a drastic circumstance overcoming our civilization, or planet, that within the next one hundred years, these words, quark, meson, and cosmic rays, will have been broken down to the language of the layman.

By the element being connected with the planetary system, it

THE EVOLUTIONIST III

opens our minds to understand that the element is in the same stage as our galaxy, just smaller. In other words, an element is made up of so many small atomic planets (protons, electrons, and neutrons) buzzing around in their own galaxy inside of different elements, which are interlocked in these orbits to form a mass of matter, which together create organisms of different beings. The organism is, to us, or the layman, a fairly recognizable being.

Five hundred years ago, the word organism was very similar to how we interact today with the words quark, meson and cosmic ray.

It is impossible for any person today to understand, who does not believe, or chooses to call these facts a lie. We are, and probably will always be, on the edge of understanding the complete story forever. However, our understanding is now in a position of just what this word "understanding" means. We have a factual foundation, and under-standing. Something that cannot be taken away. Not a myth, a fact. We are now on a solid road to Heaven!

THE EVOLUTIONIST III

𝔄nthropo is a word which means, an animal which walks on two feet in a upright position, with a bearded face. This animal may be covered with hair on the body, completely or partially.

If you add centric to anthropo, you have the word anthropocentric, which describes this upright figure as a man, and as the central fact, or final aim of the universe.

Both anthropo and centric are from the Greek language. I have often wondered why the Greek language never included the black anthropo or the orange anthropo, or the yellow anthropo, as central figures for which the universe was constructed. Maybe the Grecian population never knew anything about these others at that time, or really didn't want to hear anything about them. The words, barbarians, savages, and cannibals covered those they knew nothing about.

THE EVOLUTIONIST III

One of the first things a person is taught is that you must not build your home on a foundation of sand. The foundation of anything must be solid, in order for that which is built on top of it to last. This same rule must be applied to thought. If there is a weakness in the foundation of a certain thought, then it is necessary to reconstruct the thought on a satisfactory foundation. This must be repeated until you gain confidence that the foundation will stand the pressure of future expansion.

In turn, that expansion results in an answer that can be used for the future foundation, or for an answer to a future question.

THE EVOLUTIONIST III

All of the mystic fables that are told about Jesus bring disgust to the minds of those who know the real truth about Him. What He said was what people wanted to hear, not how He walked on water, or ascended to Heaven to stand beside God.

THE EVOLUTIONIST III

𝔜our Soul is that part of you that reflects your history.

THE EVOLUTIONIST III

You want eternity, you've got it. Throughout your life, you ricochet off the others who are just like you, and you watch the action of all creation as you live your life. What you like, you copy, and what you don't like, you handle as chaff. Every moment you spend in the spiral of life is taken advantage of by others of creation who are just as you, questioning existence. Existence is digestion of what you witness and absorb. Others, in turn, witness your actions along with the rest of creation, and winnow out what they feel not to be of value at the time or in the future.

It is impossible for anyone or anything to live life without subscribing to what they like and dislike. This same plan holds true for all creation. Transfiguration takes place to create. Creation exists as a plan for betterment.

What is better for one is not always better for the other. In this way, nothing is missed by what is presented to all. Your existence is being continually digested by those who see or hear what you say and do. Everything in creation, seen or unseen, is of value to existence. In this way, your life in never wasted. The future carries the plans and dreams for all, you are born to be forever, by living through total creation. In other words, the actions of all creation are continually being stirred into this stew we call creation. There is a touch of everything that has existed in the make up of life, and this plan has never changed; it's called evolution.

THE EVOLUTIONIST III

In the past I wrote about chasing your meal in our prehistoric history. In this paper I mentioned those who hogged the food. During this time none of us were specialists. We had to supply our own total needs for our survival by ourselves. Today we are specialists, each supplies a certain need to others for compensation to pay for the necessities of life. No one does everything; except a farmer with a milk cow to help him.

THE EVOLUTIONIST III

The mind of today has theorized the hypothesis of the inheritance of characteristics, just as Moses chiseled the commandments on tablets of stone thousands of years ago. Ancient belief of the Hy-Lo Ideals has also brought to life, in the mind of creation, that all matter is animated. Life is ever-enduring through its own principle of animation, yet there are some who still visualize as immobile, and without sensations, many parts of creation.

Physical form, force, and their mental construction have been, and still are, in the process of development. Through this physical and mental development we have learned to refer to this as the process of physical and mental evolution. Evolution means the process of progress, or change from simple to a more complex form, both physically and mentally. This statement covers, or explains, a development of the physical bodies as well as the simple-to-complex intelligence of mind.

Time spent in the investigation and study of physical being and mental inquisitiveness has rewarded creation with a sound foundation in both our physical and mental make-up. To genuinely conceive questions regarding life and its construction in their own minds, and to physically be able to ask questions concerning this life could be the most valued asset of all of our creation. In other words, it is one thing to conceive the question, but it is entirely a different situation when it comes to actually being able to speak aloud and ask the question in many different languages, and then to expect, and

THE EVOLUTIONIST III

receive an answer from others.

To more fully understand evolution it might be best to mention a few things through which we can see as an actual fact, that life and its operation are going forward through the process of both physical and mental evolution. Dress might be considered as a proper place to begin, and then we might consider travel, housing, speech, protection, pleasures, medical, and dentistry administration. We might say too, the manners of speech and the methods of communication. Lets first consider dress. Dress has never been used as a means to cover sin. Primitive dress was without doubt, in my mind, used as a means of warmth. Secondly, I would consider dress or covering the body a means of protection. Third we might consider the fact that these "cloths" we wrapped up in were in a way a transportable home. That's quite a difference from our insulated and air conditioned homes of today. Travel is very simple to recognize as being greatly improved. In our beginning, to travel as an amoebae consisted of only drifting. Then came swimming and walking or perhaps flying. Today we are flying through the universe at thousands of miles an hour. Speech went from different vocal sounds to may languages. Protection has been improved from rocks and clubs to the atomic bomb. Pleasures have passed through thousands of things considered as fun, and yet today, as always, our infants of all creation seem to get the greatest joy out of frolicking with one another. Dentistry, I can imagine to be one of our most valued improvements. We all know how a tooth can ache.

THE EVOLUTIONIST III

Medicine needs no explanation. Today we are transplanting body organs and parts. Through these few words none can say we have not evolved for the better with little change. True, our skeletal form has changed but not as far as our being able to notice a change. Our mentality has zoomed ahead like a rocket. Perhaps the skeleton that our flesh surrounds has changed little, however it has taken billions of years to stand where it now stands. and change is in effect. Physical evolution is a very slow process.

If evolution were not in the lead, or at the point of a search for the answer to being, then it must be that evolution is receiving, from another, directions to follow and reach the castle of achievement, which is being created. In other words are we in search, or are we being led or educated towards a reward? Is creation assimilating life? Or is life assimilating creation? It appears as though our morals have been driven towards obedience for protection of our being.

An attitude of vengeance can only produce vacancy. Vacancy has no desire. The mind, to be, must carry with it stalwart authority, and contain an influence which produces that which we desire most, life. The direction of this desire might be achieved through several methods. The one we have chosen to believe, so far, has been to accept life as a gift from a thing, up to this time, only mentally visualized, which has the answer we are in search of, and which at the proper time will expose to us our future with life eternal. An answer which will eliminate all future questions and present each with

THE EVOLUTIONIST III

fulfillment of all mental desires.

If this is correct, there will be no future to life, which is the fountain of desires. Our desires have been conceived as a source to remain alive, with life. Not to seek and accept a life which shall reinstill in us another desire to be. On the other hand, we might accept a way of being which steadily improves, and presents life's rewards as it lives, and also lets all who have, and will, live in a future. Being which continues to Be as it progresses in its efforts to keep life alive.

The method It has used so far seems to fill the vacancy or void we struggle to avoid. This method has been to service that which has been developed so far, in the exact way life has been serviced to get it to the point at which it now stands. This process has been a difficult one, and yet it has survived through its many problems, even with mass destruction, and physical losses which are indescribable. Our natural history is loaded with these circumstances and our future will, I'm sure, present many, many more of these near annihilations. Gazing into the universe presents an idea of what our future presents. However our journey up until now has presented us with what we have felt to be insurmountable problems which we have, and will continue to have and will continue to overcome as best we are able to. We have passed through, and will continue to pass through these problems. The cosmic entities which first placed us here, on what we call earth, will continue to retain their ability to supply us with a future, and will also continue the evolutionary progress as long as we contain the mental desire we have for life.

THE EVOLUTIONIST III

These same cosmic entities are bombarding the entire universe with the same materials with which they created our solar system. And just as when we took up traveling on our planet and were exposed to creatures we had no way of conceiving, so it will be when we take off for interplanetary exploration. However, as I have mentioned before, we must keep in mind, all that we see is still a part of us.

THE EVOLUTIONIST III

All together, Creation makes up the intelligence of One. It seems to answer to many names, and yet it is only seen by one looking at another.

THE EVOLUTIONIST III

All creation, when placed together as one, make up both the physical shape and mental intelligence of this entity we refer to as God.

THE EVOLUTIONIST III

If there are many shapes, shades, and sizes of planets; many shapes, shades, and sizes of trees; many shapes, shades, and sizes of fish; many shapes, shades, and sizes of monkeys; many shapes, shades, and sizes of plants; many shapes, shades, and sizes of ants; many shapes, shades, and sizes of snakes; then it is a positive thing that there are many shapes, shades, and sizes of humans.

The reason that all are constructed of the same materials and all operate through the same brain is to satisy the same desire for life.

THE EVOLUTIONIST III

Immortality is life which lives and passes through Being without ending. Fire burns life into life. Appearance merely satisfies the appetite of desire. Life lives without being recognized, or even seen.

THE EVOLUTIONIST III

Belief and understanding; one freed in life, relaxed, compassionate, and with knowledge permeating from the depth of the soul to the outer limits of the body, and wise with the concentration of the heart, and seeing that all things are with equal regard and beholding themselves in all Beings, and a positive reaction that all Being form a Creation together which form the mind and body of the One they have eternally existed within.

THE EVOLUTIONIST III

What is undying or imperishable, and what is transient or ephemeral, harmoniously live together. They are not, as you feel, one, and yet they cannot exist, one without the other. The mind must give them form.

THE EVOLUTIONIST III

That which is wrong, is also right, the realm of Becoming could be explained by the word death.

THE EVOLUTIONIST III

Those who have enlisted themselves, and are able to concede to the spiritual truth that the everlasting lives through them, and are also able to comprehend, and be aware of the fact that all things, if viewed as One, make up the Everlasting, which is the soul and body of eternity.

THE EVOLUTIONIST III

The plants, rocks, fire, water, with all, are life. They watch and listen to check the needs of one another. They understand through mind when others face trouble, and it is then that they reveal themselves and offer assistance.

THE EVOLUTIONIST III

How is it that we have not a word which defines any who are bisexual, by this I refer to those who contain both sexes, male and female. Even though the word "hydra" comes near, none seem to elaborate the benefits of containing both sexes, even though all creation seems to pass through this single celled Being.

THE EVOLUTIONIST III

All things, in the light of others, merely shuffle, and add to the foundation that makes up the ONE who has furnished our past, and presents our future.

THE EVOLUTIONIST III

Even the body desperately attempts reconstruction as the descendant of those whose love was created to live as one.

THE EVOLUTIONIST III

Mythology of the virgin birth is rooted in the mind of humankind as a result of impressions from their first sight of birth. Birth is the contribution to brain by adding the question, HOW?

THE EVOLUTIONIST III

Ten thousand years ago, as each generation passed there was very little way of knowing what had taken place in the generations before. Yes, there were drawings on the walls of caves, but a written language wasn't even envisioned. These same characters on the walls of the caves were, and still are, in existence today. Perhaps there was a language in existence, however the descriptive words were very limited. Undoubtedly physical signs and body language were used more than speech.

As time progressed, language was developed to a point of almost exclusively being a method of conversing, or telling a tale of history or mythology.

Today we have all sorts of ways of preserving our past history. However these methods we are using are still not capable of being a forever way of preserving our past. Each written volume, all film, the statues and paintings, and any other means of history has to be in some way reconstructed. So far, even though we can now store it, it still has to be renewed in a more lasting way. Nothing seems to last forever, not even the pictures in the caves. Thousands of generations have joined these pages of time.

One thing which we will be able to retain from our past is knowledge. Knowledge has presented us with an understanding of being able to live together in peace and security. Soon wars will only be history and our governments will hopefully be run by the multitudes in a truthful manner, in all countries.

THE EVOLUTIONIST III

The High-Low Ideals of Naden and Lewins have always been and always will be a goal, and this goal is getting closer and closer. Soon it will be fact.

THE EVOLUTIONIST III

One day, while I was in the outfitting business in Cooke City, Montana, I decided to pack into the Beartooth Wilderness to fish for Golden Trout. I asked my wife, Maxine, if she would like to go, and so we loaded up and took off in the truck filled with horses and gear. We drove east on the Beartooth highway for about twenty miles and pulled off on the Clay Butte road. We wound up the road for a mile or so, and then parked the truck and loaded up.

It took us a couple of hours to ride into Cliff Lake, where I had caught Goldens before. We unloaded the gear, put the tent up, and prepared to spend a day or so. I purposely left the horses untied while we fished. I figured they would like the fresh grass over the hay they had been eating back at the pack station. It seems that my theory was wrong. After fishing for a while, I decided that maybe I had better picket the horses and not leave them loose any longer. I guess I waited too long, for both Buck and Cinnamon were gone. I walked down the creek looking to see if they had gone for water, but no such luck.

Maxine and I got a few things together, put the saddles and gear in the tent and took off on foot to see if we could catch up with them. It took us quite a while to get back to the truck and the horses were no where around. So we headed back to Cooke City and the pack station.

The next morning, I loaded my horse, Red, into the truck and went back to where we had parked. I chose Red because he

THE EVOLUTIONIST III

was a quick moving sorrel gelding I rode when I had to travel fast. I covered a lot of ground in a few hours but could see no track and no sight of the two horses. For several days I searched the area, driving back and forth each day. It was late fall, and could start snowing at anytime. If the snow came in heavy, no telling where they would wander. One day, a friend, who was the photographer for Yellowstone Park, told me he had seen a couple of horses up around Clay Butte, but he said it was a Palomino, and a Black. Buck was a Claybank, and Cinnamon was a Bay, which could be close.

I took off one more time with Red in the truck and drove to where we had parked before. I could see horse tracks around where the truck had been, so I followed them until a storm started, and it was a bad one. I headed back for town once more. The next day, I went back. There was about a foot of snow on the ground, and once again I could see fresh tracks around where the truck had been parked. This time I went on foot, following the tracks. I trailed them for about a mile, and went over the top of Clay Butte. I looked down the other side and there they were. It looked like Shangri La down where they were scratching in the snow and eating. They had moved right into the spot, and probably figured they were set for winter. Little did they know, the snow gets about ten feet deep around there in the winter.

I walked down the butte to where they were, and climbed on Buck and we started out. I could see their tracks which they had

THE EVOLUTIONIST III

made early that morning. I followed them and they lead up to the edge of the butte where they could see where the truck was parked. I then understood what they had been doing. Some days, they just walked up to the edge of the ridge and looked over to see if the truck was there. Other days they had walked clear over to where the truck had been parked when we first went into the lake fishing. Evidently, my friend happened to see them on a day when they had come back to where the truck had been parked.

The next day, after parking the truck, I rode back into the lake and packed out the tent and gear we had left at the lake. It was pretty smart of Buck and Cinnamon to check each day to see if I had come back to get them, and I'm sure they felt like they were set for the winter, if I didn't. Little did they know they would have frozen through the winter and would become food for the Grizzlies the next spring.

Buck lived about ten years after that excursion, and Cinnamon is almost thirty-five now and is on pasture just a few miles from Kernville, where I put this story together.

THE EVOLUTIONIST III

Just for something to think about. In order to look a little cooler, our ancestors learned to cook the flesh of the other animals we ate. By doing this the flesh became much more tender and we no longer needed fangs to tear it apart. Consequently our fangs slowly receded into what we call "canine teeth".

"Canine" makes us feel that we are "different" from those who still have "fangs".

THE EVOLUTIONIST III

I stand convinced in my belief in evolution. To me, both physical and mental evolution are reality, and have placed us in the position we now claim. This position is a full relationship to all, both Spiritual and Materialistic which present us together as One, which creates the essence of life, which we live through.

THE EVOLUTIONIST III

Physical appearance has nothing to do with the mental capabilities of any of creation. It is true that many times both brain and physical appearance are affected at birth. An example, although fictitious, the Hunchback of Notre Dame.

THE EVOLUTIONIST III

Permeation still exists in the bodies of creation, just as it does in the single cell. Perspiration works both ways.

THE EVOLUTIONIST III

𝔄ll are destined to reflect their thoughts. Thoughts create thoughts, and expose themselves through the permeation of actions. Words are not necessary, and cannot control our reactions to life. Thoughts require nourishment just as flesh, and expose themselves in the same manner. Those who are able to control the reactions of their body come closer to being able to control the exposure of their thoughts. However, no matter what control one possesses, thoughts continue to leak into existence, and there are others who continually take advantage of the thoughts of others, and who add them to their personal burden of secrets, which will soon seep into existence once again.

THE EVOLUTIONIST III

If humankind, as a part of Creation, can create a transmitter that sends and accepts messages, and then improve it to also include the ability to send and receive pictures, don't you feel that this Creator, who constructed everything, could do the same thing, and even make it out of flesh? When it comes down to it, that is exactly what has been taking place. There's only one difference. The Creator made the thing out of flesh first, and then had the thing made out of flesh make the transmitter.

THE EVOLUTIONIST III

If we cannot separate ourselves from life, then we must be a continual part of what is creating life.

THE EVOLUTIONIST III

Today it's possible for humankind to visualize their past, from the days of riding horses or walking as the only means of travel, to being able to fly in airplanes, float the high sea in giant cruise ship, or ride in motorized vehicles at great speeds. In my memory bank, which is a little over seventy five years old, I can remember riding in cars that I thought were the greatest, that were really only a step above a horse drawn wagon. It took us nearly three weeks to drive from the San Fernando Valley to Des Moines, Iowa, most of the way on dirt roads. My past was just a short time in history from the days of the last frontier.

In just a short time we will, or let's put it this way, our younger generation will be able to see as fact our past. I, myself, can visualize living in a log cabin, in Montana, pumping water by hand and heating the log house with a wood fire and cooking on a wood stove. Using an out-house toilet, eating jerked elk and deer that I shot,and boiling soaked beans for dinner.

By seeing and living through these early years it was easy for me to look into my past and feel what it really represented. Very few people could read, and less could write. X was a common way to sign one's name. Nights were spent entertaining one another by singing or telling wild west stories. I can remember many times sitting around in the evening listening to these sort of tales. This represents our past with a foundation for us which can be handed down as truth.

THE EVOLUTIONIST III

Certain things that have happened, that have provided answers to the way we are put together, should be put in text for our future use.

Such is the case of Linneous Finnegan. An accident he had resulted in a one-inch by thirty-inch steel rod being driven through his brain without killing him. This brought on early discoveries concerning how brain functions.

Many of our vital discoveries concerning the bodies of all creation have been the results of accidents, which happened to our different bodies, and perhaps speed up evolutionary reaction.

THE EVOLUTIONIST III

It appears as though the multitudes would have no problem settling their problems. The real problem is with the leaders of the multitudes, who want more than peace and understanding.

THE EVOLUTIONIST III

"Let there be light"? Life began before light and darkness came!

THE EVOLUTIONIST III

Instant generation, and as quick, a life. We, in almost our smallest physically-generated bodies, exist as the speed of light. Faster than sight. Yet, there are those who continue to wonder.

THE EVOLUTIONIST III

When it comes down to it, really, there is no reason to ask. When you do, you are creating a problem for yourself. If you do ask, what difference will the answer make? You still have to decide for yourself, "Is this answer correct?"

THE EVOLUTIONIST III

I feel I have finally answered, for myself, what an animal is. When it is used in the context of science: anything which is constructed, and responsive. Simply, taken as alive, or referred to as a flame.

THE EVOLUTIONIST III

When eyes first gazed at the universe that surrounds our planet, mythology was conceived.

THE EVOLUTIONIST III

When you make a phone call you are setting in motion another part of yourself to carry out an order. This order could be in many ways or forms. Compensation is given on your part, for this extension of your desires to pass through another being. This is the exposition of evolution.

THE EVOLUTIONIST III

No matter how far we go, or how close we get, there's still another step. Sometimes, it has to wait until tomorrow.

THE EVOLUTIONIST III

Convulsion is a necessity for generation and, undoubtedly, evolution is satisfied through generation.

THE EVOLUTIONIST III

𝕴t all started while I was reading Ernst Haeckel's, History of Creation, Vol. II, page 408. While discussing an Indian Gibbon (Hylobates Agilis) Haeckel stated that, "the Indian Gibbon, the singing apes, stand as far above the American Howling Apes, as the nightingale stands above the crow."

This Indian Gibbon drew my attention, and I waded into my twenty-five thousand pages of Oxford Dictionaries to find out what I could about this singing ape "man".

My first thought was to investigate the Hylobates. On checking, there wasn't any such word under that headings, and so I settled for hylo-. In the Oxford English Dictionary, there are many reference words to hylo-, and the first one that caught my eye was, in 1883 Constance Naden stated, "many cherished illusions must fall when the Hylo-Ideal theory is finally established". In 1823 Webster, "Hulotheism, the doctrine or belief that matter is God, or that there is no God except matter and the universe". Lorenz Oken, 1779-1851, explains that Hylogeny is the doctrine of material totalities. 1884 Cassell's Encyclical Dictionary, the central insistence of the Hylo-Ideal philosophy is that man, for man, is the measure of the universe. During the 1890's, Dr. Lewins was teaching a philosophical creed called Hylo-Idealism. In 1881 Saint Thomas held or adhered to a Hylo-Morphical system.

Through those who expressed their views on Hylo - you can see that there has been much discussion, and through many

THE EVOLUTIONIST III

languages, on the subject, or thoughts that concern this ancient philosophy.

My own feelings have leaned towards these same thoughts before I ever came in contact with the Hylobates Agilis monkey.

Perhaps, in reality, humankind are worshiping themselves and the rest of creation, when they worship what they call, or refer to as, God.

It looks like I hit the motherload when I stumbled on to the word Hylo. I couldn't believe the results so far. And now I decided to check words out with similar spelling. I opened the <u>Oxford Dictionary, Volume III</u>, to page 584 and there was the word Hyle; Hylo's cousin.

It seems like fate, or perhaps something leading me to make it possible for me to be encouraged by what is being opened up to me.

As some of you have read my papers, you have understood how I feel about our cosmic being, no matter their shape or substance, as having passed through the flames of being. Now I'm shown the word Hyle. Aristotle used a Greek word to explain the same thing Hyle meant; wood, timber, material, substance; the first matter of the universe. In 1390, they called material, universal. 1400, they said secret. 1619, Uncreated Chaos, or Hyla, or first matter. 1652, this hyle or matter is indeed nothing else but the souls potentiality. 1687, Hyle, or first matter, is mere possibility of Being, according to Aristotle. 1768-74, Tucker (1852) i. 464, Jove

THE EVOLUTIONIST III

produced the two first numbers, the mundane soul and hyle: he made hyle inert and stupid, but to mundane soul he gave activity and understanding.

Chaos, potentiality on one side, stupidity the opposite.

Hyloist is one that affirms that matter is God. Huloist, the same as Hyloist.

For now, at last we are <u>ALL</u> able to see God: Universal Creation through the simple word, Hylo.

In 1678, Cudworth wrote, Hylozoism made all body as such, and therefore, every smallest Atom of it, to have life essentially belonging to it. In 1887, R. D. Hicks wrote in the <u>Encyclopedia Britannica, Volume XXII</u>, pages 562-3, to Cleanths and Chrysippus. There was no real difference between matter and its cause. They have reached the final result of unveiled hylozoism.

In 1678, Cudworth spoke, "As every Atomist is not therefore necessarily an Atheist, so neither must every Hylozoist needs be accounted such."

During this period of time the word evolution was beginning to display its head. Also, evolution was more controllable than having everyone and everything represent a God you could actually see. Due to the heavy convictions of those who opposed Hylo and the meaning it carries with it, to argue over evolution was much easier than opposing a God that was made up of the entire universe. Hylo was left to seclusion, hidden in a maze of simple words that appeared meaningless and harmless.

THE EVOLUTIONIST III

I'm sure that Constance Naden enjoys seeing her Hylo-Ideal theory brought out of the seclusion it has been in for the past one hundred and sixteen years. Maybe the cherished illusions will tumble, as the Tower of Babel, sooner than most thought.

THE EVOLUTIONIST III

Have mankind forced evolution? Or have mankind been a result of evolution? Out of the west came a beast swinging a club. The club has evolved to become atomic energy: mankind's sparks become greater and greater each day. How far shall we go?

THE EVOLUTIONIST III

I've had the feeling most of my life, that it was necessary for humankind to create a means of travel to permit themselves to journey from planet to planet in order to carry on the accomplishments we have made or created here on earth. Also this would be a means by which we could preserve the accomplishments we have achieved in our physical evolution.

It has taken us billions of years to pass through this physical and mental evolutionary process, and it would be a shame to lose all we have achieved by being stranded on this planet, we describe as Earth, only to perish. However, I can see now that our past has been just as satisfactory to us in the physical stage we were in, as what will be ours in the physical shape we may carry in the future.

Live today and satisfy yourself as you accept what lies in the future. It is impossible to remove or erase memories; make the memories as pleasant as you can. Take advantage of what you feel to be a drastic situation: we will meet again!

THE EVOLUTIONIST III

As humankind gaze into the universal space today, as they have for the past billion or so years, it is an entirely different mental vision. In the past, as we related ourselves to the rest of creation, we envisioned only spots in the night's darkness, no not even stars. As daylight presented itself these stars were replace by sunlight, and nightfall presented itself once again, and once again these same spots appeared. There was no magic or god which made them reappear, and truly why ask for a reason. They just came with the darkness as an automatic happening. This same scene took place every night just as the thunder and rain presented itself when their time arose. There was no magic to life as it presented itself to creation daily. We came into being and passed on into the wilderness of the unknown just as the rest of creation does today. A thing the human race can no longer take for granted; today they have to know, why?

    Why is it that only us humans have to know? What is the reason that we must understand something that in our past we didn't only accept as a part of life as it unfolded itself to us, but we had no way of even contriving a desire to know. We lived by our wit, which we never realized we even had.

    Then something came about which made us realize that we had learned to copy the actions of the rest of creation that surrounded us and the rules of nature that brought the unexpected light. We began taking advantage of what we saw others of creation doing. Instead of living continually in a cave we watched as a bird thatched a nest, or a beaver stopped the flow of a stream by creating a dam, or an otter smash a clam while laying on his back with a rock, used as an anvil resting on his stomach. And as we copied their actions we slowly began to feel a difference, and this difference was presenting us with a feeling of being superior to that which in our past had seemed only a physical difference. Our thoughts were changing just as our physical shapes had. Without our knowing it, our forms, along with the rest of creation, had slowly been molded and remolded to allow us the advantage of being able to think and create for ourselves; a thing which would become one of our most valued assets. We were loosening our bonds and escaping into the world of the future. What might have been thought of as being smart or vogue, was more like a helgamite being transformed to a dobsonfly, or better yet, the egg into a bird. We were surging deeper into the depths of intelligence, and the further we searched, the less we understood. We were leaving serenity for sensibility, and were being presented with animation. No longer were we able to participate on an even basis with the rest of creation. We had seen no difference in our physical evolution, just as we had seen no change in the bodies of the rest of creation, which indeed we were, and still are an equal part of.

    In past history, we learned new tricks from other parts of creation as they built nests, took baths, and carried on their daily lives. Our imitation of these "others" had given us a jump start into

THE EVOLUTIONIST III

the future.

As we copied the rest of creation and accomplished both a physical and mental foundation furnished to us by them, we then slowly separated ourselves from the rest of creation. We became what we really, deeply, wanted to be, which made humankind believe that we were better than the rest of creation: we were even later told that we were the chosen!

Our egos were born. We could now be more than an equal part of creation. We would soon be known as humankind. Someone who wants to understand: to really know.

THE EVOLUTIONIST III

Man's greatest problem seems to be the awareness of having to share life with all creation, and being told that they are no better than the rest of this creation by the One they worship.

THE EVOLUTIONIST III

Just as we gazed and pondered the terrestrials, which surrounded us in our early years on planet Earth, thousands, or perhaps millions of years ago, today we gaze into the universal space in an attempt to conceive what we will see when others arrive, if they do, here on our planet Earth.

When, and if they do, will this indifference, if there is any, be understood by those who, as yet, do not understand.

THE EVOLUTIONIST III

𝔐oses and Aaron had the greatest thing ever going since the mythology of the pharaohs, and then came Constance Naden and the inkling that possibly Life Itself could be the result of what represents this Thing called God.

If this is true, then we must worship Ourselves.

THE EVOLUTIONIST III

𝕴 don't know why this thought has evaded me for so long. I have mentioned, in my writings before, about women being made gods in our early history due to their ability to produce children. I can see how this could be very easy to believe at that time, and possibly even today.

What puzzles me most is why I was passing over one of the most important connections to women being gods: the bees, and ants. Both of these species, which we might explain as animals, and related to us, have queens in their colonies. Not kings, just plain queens. They furnish the ant and bee population with their "children", and it seems to take only one of these queens for each colony, or tribe.

These queens, which we observe and gave the title of queen, never seemed to be able to achieve the title of king or God. The male, of humankind, had enough trouble breaking the noses off all the statues of the goddesses in Moses' time. They surely did not want to start it all over again, so they let the bees and ants know they had a woman queen and let's forget making her a god, too.

I've really never been able to accept the male population as being the true leaders, and God being only male. It seems we should have both. Maybe a single cell with both male and female in one body is the answer. Or possibly we should let the bisexuals handle our leadership. Come to think of it, I seem to remember this taking place in our recent history. From what I've been taught, and read,

THE EVOLUTIONIST III

there have been quite a few nations which have been ruled by persons who were attracted to both sexes.

THE EVOLUTIONIST III

Physical life is created from pure thought, after it has been conceived, digested, and excreted, by a Thing we might refer to as God.

The results of your digestion of these words, or this thought, are not intended to bring you to the conclusion that, life is a world of dung.

Another interpretation of the beginnings of physical being is that pure thought travels beyond the limits of imagination. The slag of this pure thought is the creation, or perhaps we are born from nowhere. Nowhere could be Heaven.

THE EVOLUTIONIST III

𝕴n the practice of Hinduism, a blowing out of the flame of life of the individual, or extinction of the flame of life, brings about the reunion with Brahma. Brahma, as explained in Hinduism, is the supreme and eternal essence or spirit of the universe. Also the chief member of the trinity (Brahma, Vishnu, and Siva) and creator of the universe. As always they have a stand-in, which in this case there are two, Vishnu and Siva. These are considered as standbys in case a follower asks who created Brahma. To reach Brahma a person must concede their individuality.

Buddhism is very close to Hinduism. In the case of Buddhism, when the individual reaches the state of Nirvana, it is much like Hinduism, which is represented as a blowing out, or extinction, of the flame of life through reunion with Brahma. Buddhism requires the perfect state of blessedness achieved by the extinction of individual existence and by the extinction of all desires and passions. Nirvana is achieved by being any place, or in any condition of great peace or bliss. Once again, to get there a person must concede their individuality.

Christianism, in a certain way, made it a little easier. They say, "It's easier for a camel to walk through the eye of a needle, than it is for a rich man to get into heaven". A cooler way of putting it, just don't get rich!

Materialism makes it easier than all three of the others. There is no need for you to achieve anything. Through Materialistic

THE EVOLUTIONIST III

Evolution you are already there. Everything and everyone is already a part of all. There is no individual that has to give you the right, nor do you have to achieve a certain position.Everyone and everything has it all. The rough part of evolution is over. It's steaks, Cadillacs and wild, wild times from here or out.

THE EVOLUTIONIST III

It seems like it would take some one fairly intelligent to create something as great as the universe. I don't think that what ever It is only had mankind on It's mind when the universe was created. I feel we are very lucky that we were even considered. The power used to put all of this together must be unimaginable, and just to be on the safe side, we should certainly avoid trying to be jerks.

THE EVOLUTIONIST III

Today, approximately ten thousand years after the introduction of any type of written language, humankind are more than ever anticipating the arrival of some sort of extraterrestrial beings on our planet Earth. There have been many stories about small beings visiting us in all sorts of space craft, and even such stories having to do with our people being taken for rides in their machines.

As we dwell on what we have heard about these instances, we are constantly being bombarded with all sorts of life from outer space. Terrestrial beings in all shapes and sizes are shooting at us by the billions every second, Perhaps not as large as what we refer to as man, but again as large as animals were and still are while existing in a single cell. There are those who come through space and bombard our planet which present themselves as cosmic rays, or mesons (now referred to as muons), which make up a quark, which are akin to the atom. And as most understand now, the atom is the base structure of us and includes being a part of all the universe.

There is also a tiny terrestrial creature which comes to us from the atmosphere which we can smell, taste, see, and feel. These tiny animals, which are very much animated, sacrifice themselves to the fish of the high country as one of their basic foods, so much so that the odor of these small creatures is very prevalent in the odor of both whitefish and grayling. Both of these fish (animals) are native of the northern hemisphere.

THE EVOLUTIONIST III

For many years, while traveling on foot and horseback through the high mountains of the northwest, I have come in contact with these small terrestrial beings. While in the atmosphere, they give the drifting clouds they ride on a sort of reddish-pink tint. I'm sure millions of other creatures, we call animals, have gazed at these colored clouds which contain what I have learned to call "cyclop shrimp". Nearly as much as I have seen their presence in the clouds, I have seen the snow on the high ranges covered with this same reddish-pink tint. And also I have witnessed grayling, trout, and char swim through the shallow waters of these high lakes and stir up the bottoms, exposing the same small, reddish-pink beings. After exposing them the same fish will return with their mouths open and feed on these small shrimp, just as the whales eat plankton. In the water these small shrimp are smaller than the head of a pin. In the snow they resemble small dots, and those in the atmosphere must be smaller yet.

Proof of their being is very predominant when a person drives along highway 395, in the Owens Valley, just north of Little Lake, on the way to Bishop, California. When you pass a large, dry (most of the time) lake, you can see this same reddish-pink tint all over most of the surface. The snow water which contains these reddish beings comes from the high country of Sierra Nevada Mountains and the atmosphere. These same small shrimp live in this snow water.

The positive fact of these terrestrial animals is their taste. To

THE EVOLUTIONIST III

taste them in the bed of the dry lake I just wrote about is impossible, due to the mineral salt-like taste which predominates the area. However, if a person will go to the high country snow and watch for this same pinkish-red coloring on the surface of the snow, and then taste it, they will find that this same flavor is contained in grayling and whitefish. The flavor is very easy to recognize, it tastes exactly like watermelon.

This same process of clouds carrying these small terrestrial beings and the mesons, which are a base to the atom and many more parts of our structure being furnished to us from space, has been taking place ever since the universe came into existence. Size seems to be our main concern, and time and size are both relative. Life and meaning are the real question. It seems we are learning more answers everyday.

THE EVOLUTIONIST III

Organic life beneath the shoreless waves,
   Was born and nurs'd in Ocean's pearly caves;

First forms minute, unseen by spheric glass,
   Move on the mud, or pierce the watery mass;

These, as successive generations bloom,
   New powers acquire, and larger limbs assume;

Whence countless groups of vegetation spring,
   And breathing realms of fin, and feet, and wing.
Erasmus Darwin

Now you know where Charles Darwin got the idea to expound the belief of evolution. Erasmus was the grandfather of Charles.

THE EVOLUTIONIST III

Could it have been that some of us came walking out of the sea wearing shells?

THE EVOLUTIONIST III

As smart as we feel ourselves to be today, there are still certain things in our future that seem to cause us grief. The largest of these worries is only a few months away. The year two thousand is upon us. And just as the year one was coming up two thousand years ago, today we are being pecked from all sides of our bone-covered brain, with all sorts of prophesied problems.

This time, there is no fear of a flesh-covered God. It's a plastic-covered one called the computer. Our big fear, at this time, is that this mental beast is going to cause our money to go away. Swallowed up.

As usual, the Big Boys aren't worried. Just like always, they're the swallowers.

THE EVOLUTIONIST III

In Arthur Koestler's book, The Case of the Mid-Wife Toad, Koestler states, "The neo-Darwinian theory postulates that the parents can transmit, through the channels of heredity, only what they have inherited themselves and nothing else -- none of the new acquisitions in skills or bodily features that they have made in their lifetime. One might compare this doctrine to a law which decrees that a man can leave to his heirs only what he himself had been left by his parents, neither more nor less -- not the added wealth he had acquired, nor the house he had built, not the patents of the inventions he made, nor the debts he had incurred. In so far as the matter of his offspring is concerned, he might say with Ecclesiastes that all his efforts amounted to *"vanity and chasing the wind"*. The generic endowment is transmitted down through the generations, unaffected by anything that happened to its transient carriers in their lifetime. This doctrine of *"continuity and unalterability of the germ-tract"* postulated by German zoologist August Weismann in 1885, was a cornerstone of Darwinism in Kammerer's time, 1880-1926 (Paul Kammerer being the subject of The Case of the Mid-Wife Toad), and it still is at the time of this writing. The textbooks tell us that the genetic blueprint is located in the chromosomes of the germ-cells, which are kept in splendid isolation from the rest of the body. They are potentially immoral molecular structures, protected from the hazards of life, and passed on, unaltered, from generation to generation along the *"continuous germ-tract"*. In the Lamarkian view, evolution is cumulative; in the Darwinian, repetitive; it could go on for millions of generations without any evolutionary progress.

How then did the blueprint for amoeba nevertheless become transformed into the blueprint of man? According to neo-Darwinian theory, this happened thanks to the occasional occurrence of chance events, on a microscopic scale, called *"random mutations"*. Mutations are defined as spontaneous changes in the molecular structure of the chromosomes. And they are said to be random because they are supposed to be totally unrelated to whatever goes on in the animal's environment, and thus totally unrelated to its evolutionary needs. Since they are random, most of these mutations produce harmful or lethal effects, but there must also occur from time to time a few lucky hits which offer some minute advantage on the carrier of the mutated chromosome, and this will be preserved by the operation of natural selection.

In a lecture to an audience of schoolteachers and educators, Paul Kammerer spoke of Lamarkian evolution. Frobel Pestalozzi (educational reformers much in vogue at the time) and their schools relied on the potential dispositions which the child inherits from its ancestors, hereditary dispositions which the educator hoped to enrich; but he could not hope to bestow on the children a permanent heirloom in which their children's children would be able to share -- only a gift for the fleeting duration of an individual existence. They could not conclude otherwise but that at the death of an individual, his acquired merits would also die with him. His heirs might continue what the ancestor began, but however excellent their hereditary dispositions, they again had to begin at the beginning.

However, on the hypothesis of the inheritability of acquired characteristics, which seems to be closer to the truth, the individual's efforts (according to Lamarkianism) are not wasted; they are not limited by his own lifespan, but enter into the life-sap of generations. It depends on us whether it will produce a benign or destructive effect. In other words, there are positive and negative. It's up to the individual to comprehend which is which by their own personal judgment, and guide the energy received from them in a righteous direction to satisfy their soul."

By teaching our children and pupils how to prevail in the struggles of life and attain an even higher level of perfection, we give them more than short benefits for their own lifetime -- because an extract of it will penetrate that substance which is truly the immortal part of man.

Out of the treasure of potentialities contained in the hereditary substance transmitted to us from the past, we form and transform, according to our choice and fancy, a new and better future.

When a person looks at a rabbit and then at its young, it is easy to see the resemblance. When a person looks at the father and mother of a child, it is just as easy to see the child's resemblance to the parent. If this is true, then why, too, cannot the mental structures of each be carried forth through birth, with ever-so-slight changes? This is very easy to see in our complexions, which are ever rearranging

    The voice is a perfect example of Lamarkian evolution. Many times a child will talk and sound just as their parents. This is true when a person moves from New York to Mississippi, and after a few years in their new place of inhabitancy, almost completely lose the sound of their native New York speech. Even the sound of the bark of the dog is inherited. Or the hoot of the owl is the same as its parents. It is impossible for the likeness of both physical and vocal to be the only asset of inheritance. The mind, too, has its reflections.